Quantum Computing Explained For Everyone

Applications of Quantum Computing
and Its Impact on the
Economy, Science and Everyday Life.
A Clear and Simple Guide.

Published by Tyler Soloway.

Tyler Soloway

TABLE OF CONTENTS

INTRODUCTION

Why writing this book?

Quantum computing is one of the most exciting technologies of our time, yet it remains widely misunderstood. Many people have heard of it but find it too complex or abstract to grasp. This book aims to change that.

You don't need a background in physics or computer science to understand quantum computing. This book explains it in simple terms, using clear language and everyday examples. No equations, no technical jargon—just an accessible guide to one of the most important innovations of the 21st century.

Quantum computing will impact industries, businesses, and daily life. It will revolutionize artificial intelligence, medicine, cybersecurity, and even finance. Understanding it today means being prepared for the future.

If you're curious about what quantum computing is, how it works, and why it matters, this book is for you.

Why Quantum Computing matters today?

Quantum computing is not just another advancement in technology—it is a revolution that could reshape the way we solve problems. Unlike traditional computers, which process information using bits that can be either 0 or 1, quantum computers use **qubits**, which can exist in multiple states at the same time. This allows them to perform complex calculations far faster than today's most powerful supercomputers.

But why does this matter? Because some problems are simply too difficult for classical computers to solve in a reasonable time. For example, designing new medicines, optimizing financial markets, or developing more efficient energy solutions require enormous computing power. Quantum computers have the potential to handle these challenges in ways that were previously impossible.

In cybersecurity, quantum computing could both create risks and provide new solutions. Many encryption methods that protect our data today could become obsolete, but at the same time, quantum computers could help develop new, more secure encryption techniques.

Artificial intelligence is another field that will be transformed. Quantum computing could accelerate machine learning, making AI systems smarter and more efficient. It could also lead to breakthroughs in materials science, helping researchers discover new materials for batteries, electronics, and even space exploration.

Although quantum computers are still in their early stages, their potential impact is enormous. Understanding quantum computing today means preparing for a future where it will play a key role in science, business, and daily life.

How to read the book?

This book is designed to be easy to follow, whether you want to read it from start to finish or jump directly to the topics that interest you most. Each chapter explores a key aspect of quantum computing in a clear and simple way, without requiring any prior knowledge.

If you are new to the subject, reading the book in order will help you gradually build an understanding of quantum computing, from basic concepts to its real-world applications. However, if you are curious about a specific topic—such as how quantum computing will impact cybersecurity or artificial intelligence—you can skip ahead to the relevant chapter without missing important context.

The goal is to make learning about quantum computing an enjoyable and accessible experience. Take your time, explore the ideas, and most importantly, have fun discovering the future of technology!

1. WHAT IS QUANTUM COMPUTING?

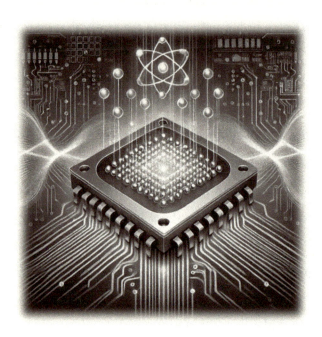

Basic principles of quantum mechanics

To understand quantum computing, we first need to explore the strange world of **quantum mechanics**—the science that describes how tiny particles, like atoms and electrons, behave. Unlike objects in our everyday world, these particles follow a completely different set of rules, which can seem counterintuitive at first.

One of the most important ideas in quantum mechanics is **superposition**. In the classical world, a light switch is either ON or OFF, and a coin is either heads or tails. But in the quantum world, a particle can exist in **multiple states at the same time**. This means that a quantum computer, instead of working with bits that are strictly 0 or 1, uses **qubits** that can be both 0 and 1 simultaneously. This ability allows quantum computers to process vast amounts of information at once.

Another key concept is **entanglement**, a mysterious link between particles. When two particles become entangled, their states are connected no matter how far apart they are. If one particle changes, the other reacts instantly, even if they are on opposite sides of the universe. This strange connection could lead to powerful advances in computing and secure communication.

Quantum mechanics also introduces the idea of **probability**. In classical physics, if you know all the conditions of a system, you can predict its future with certainty. But in quantum mechanics, things are different. Instead of fixed outcomes, we deal with probabilities. A quantum system does not settle on a definite state until it is observed, a phenomenon known as the **observer effect**.

These principles may seem strange, but they are the foundation of quantum computing. By using **superposition, entanglement, and probability**, quantum computers operate in ways that classical computers never could, opening the door to revolutionary possibilities.

How quantum computing differs from traditional computing

To understand quantum computing, it helps to compare it with traditional computing, the type of computing we use every day in smartphones, laptops, and servers. While both process information, they do so in fundamentally different ways.

Traditional computers operate using **bits**, the smallest unit of data, which can be either **0 or 1**. Every calculation, from opening an app to running complex simulations, is performed by manipulating billions of these bits in sequences of zeros and ones. This binary system is efficient and reliable, but it has limits, especially when tackling extremely complex problems that require enormous computing power.

Quantum computers, on the other hand, use **qubits** (quantum bits), which follow the rules of **quantum mechanics**. Unlike classical bits, qubits can exist in a state of **superposition**, meaning they can be both **0 and 1 at the same time**. This allows quantum computers to process many possibilities simultaneously, making them incredibly powerful for certain types of calculations.

Another key difference is **entanglement**, a unique property of quantum mechanics. When qubits become entangled, their states are linked, even if they are separated by vast distances. This enables quantum computers to perform complex computations more efficiently than classical computers, which must process information step by step.

Because of these properties, quantum computers are not just **faster** versions of classical computers. Instead, they are a **completely new type of computing**, capable of solving certain problems—like breaking encryption, simulating molecules for drug discovery, and optimizing complex systems—far beyond the reach of today's most powerful supercomputers.

However, quantum computing is still in its early stages. The technology is delicate, requiring extremely low temperatures and precise conditions to function correctly. While traditional computers remain the best choice for everyday tasks, quantum computers will eventually revolutionize fields that rely on solving highly complex problems.

A brief history of quantum computing

The idea of quantum computing is rooted in the early 20th century when scientists began to uncover the strange and fascinating rules of **quantum mechanics**. Unlike classical physics, which describes the world we see around us, quantum mechanics deals with the behavior of particles at the smallest scales—atoms and subatomic particles—which follow rules that seem counterintuitive.

One of the pioneers of quantum theory was **Max Planck**, who, in 1900, introduced the idea that energy is not continuous but comes in small, discrete packets called **quanta**. A few years later, **Albert Einstein** built on this concept to explain the photoelectric effect, which earned him the Nobel Prize. As scientists explored these ideas further, they discovered even stranger properties, such as **superposition** and **entanglement**, which would later become the foundation of quantum computing.

In the 1980s, the idea of using quantum mechanics for computing began to take shape. **Richard Feynman**, a renowned physicist, suggested in 1981 that quantum systems could be simulated more efficiently using quantum computers rather than classical ones. Around the same time, **David Deutsch** developed the concept of a **universal quantum computer**, proving that such a machine could, in theory, perform any computation that a classical computer could—only much faster for certain tasks.

The 1990s brought significant progress. **Peter Shor**, a mathematician at Bell Labs, developed an algorithm that could use quantum computing to break encryption systems that protect much of today's digital information. This discovery demonstrated that quantum computers, if built successfully, could surpass classical computers in critical areas like cybersecurity. Around the same time, **Lov Grover** developed a quantum algorithm for searching databases much faster than any classical method.

As technology advanced, researchers and companies started building the first **real** quantum computers. In the early 2000s, experimental quantum processors were created using **superconducting circuits**, laying the foundation for modern quantum computing hardware. By the 2010s, major companies like **IBM, Google, Microsoft, and startups like D-Wave** had invested heavily in quantum computing, each racing to build more stable and powerful quantum machines.

In 2019, Google claimed to have achieved **quantum supremacy**, meaning their quantum computer performed a specific task faster than the most powerful classical supercomputer could. While this was a significant milestone, quantum computing is still in its infancy. Today, researchers continue working to improve the **stability, scalability, and practical applications** of quantum computers.

The journey of quantum computing is still unfolding, but one thing is clear: this technology has the potential to revolutionize fields like **medicine, artificial intelligence, materials science, and cybersecurity**. While it may take years before quantum computers become widely used, the progress made so far suggests that the future of computing will look very different from today.

2. CHALLENGES FOR QUANTUM COMPUTING

Technological hurdles

Quantum computing is a fascinating and promising field, but building a functional quantum computer comes with enormous challenges. Unlike classical computers, which use well-established technologies like transistors and silicon chips, quantum computers require entirely new materials, techniques, and engineering solutions.

One of the biggest hurdles is **qubit stability**. Traditional computers store information in bits, which can be either 0 or 1. Quantum computers, on the other hand, use **qubits**, which can exist in a state of **superposition**, meaning they can be both 0 and 1 at the same time. However, qubits are incredibly fragile. Any small disturbance from the outside world—such as temperature changes, electromagnetic radiation, or vibrations—can cause them to lose their quantum state in a process called **decoherence**. This makes it extremely difficult to maintain the accuracy of calculations.

To keep qubits stable, quantum computers must operate in extreme conditions. Many of today's quantum machines are kept at temperatures close to **absolute zero** (-273°C or -459°F), making them some of the coldest places in the universe. These freezing temperatures help reduce noise and interference, but they also require complex refrigeration systems, which are expensive and difficult to maintain.

Another challenge is **error correction**. In classical computing, errors can be detected and corrected using standard techniques. In quantum computing, error correction is far more complicated because measuring a qubit destroys its quantum state. Scientists have developed **quantum error correction codes**, but these require using multiple physical qubits to represent a single "logical" qubit. This means that to build a large, useful quantum computer, we would need **millions of physical qubits** just to create a few thousand reliable qubits. Currently, the best quantum computers only have a few hundred qubits, which is far from the scale needed for practical applications.

Building a large-scale quantum computer also requires solving the problem of **qubit connectivity**. In classical computers, transistors are connected in circuits that allow fast communication between different parts of the processor. In quantum computers, qubits must be carefully arranged and entangled in a way that allows efficient calculations. This is incredibly difficult because increasing the number of qubits makes it harder to control them and prevent errors from spreading.

Another major hurdle is **scalability**. Researchers have been able to build small quantum processors, but scaling them up to thousands or millions of qubits is an enormous engineering challenge. The more qubits a system has, the more complex the wiring, cooling, and control mechanisms become. Some companies are experimenting with different designs, such as **trapped ions, superconducting qubits, and photonic quantum computers**, to find the best approach. However, no single method has proven to be the ultimate solution yet.

Beyond hardware, **software development for quantum computing** is still in its early stages. Writing programs for quantum computers requires new programming languages and algorithms that take advantage of quantum mechanics. Since quantum computing works very differently from classical computing, developers need to rethink how to design software from the ground up. Today, companies like IBM, Google, and Microsoft are creating tools to make quantum programming more accessible, but widespread adoption is still years away.

Finally, quantum computers require **a reliable way to integrate with existing technology**. Even if we build a powerful quantum machine, it will not replace classical computers but rather work alongside them. Finding efficient ways to transfer data between quantum and classical systems is another challenge that must be solved before quantum computers can be used in everyday applications.

Despite these technological hurdles, researchers are making progress every year. Many experts believe that, within a few decades, we will overcome these challenges and unlock the full potential of quantum computing. Until then, the journey continues, with scientists and engineers pushing the boundaries of what is possible.

The need for new materials and infrastructure

Quantum computers are not just more powerful versions of classical computers. They require completely different materials, components, and environments to function. Unlike traditional computers, which are built using silicon chips and standard electronic circuits, quantum computers rely on delicate quantum properties that demand entirely new types of hardware. This presents a significant challenge because the materials and infrastructure needed to build large-scale quantum systems do not yet exist in a practical, cost-effective form.

One of the most pressing challenges is **finding the right materials for qubits**. In classical computers, transistors made from silicon reliably process billions of calculations per second. In quantum computing, however, qubits must be made from materials that can maintain quantum states such as **superposition** and **entanglement**. Several approaches are being explored, including superconducting circuits, trapped ions, photons, and even exotic states of matter called **topological qubits**. Each method has its advantages and drawbacks, but no single material has proven to be the best solution for building a scalable quantum computer.

Superconducting qubits, for example, require metals that can conduct electricity without resistance at extremely low temperatures. This means that quantum processors must be housed in special refrigerators called **dilution refrigerators**, which cool them down to temperatures near absolute zero (-273°C or -459°F). These refrigerators are large, expensive, and difficult to maintain, making it impractical to deploy quantum computers on a wide scale using today's technology.

Trapped ion qubits, another promising approach, use individual atoms suspended in vacuum chambers and manipulated with lasers. While these qubits can be highly stable, they require **complex optical systems** to control them, making the hardware bulky and difficult to scale. Other methods, such as **photonic quantum computing**, rely on specially engineered light particles, but these require advanced materials that can precisely guide and control photons without significant loss of information.

In addition to qubit materials, quantum computing also demands **new types of wiring and circuit designs**. Traditional wires and electronic components generate heat and electrical noise, which can interfere with the fragile quantum states of qubits. To minimize these disturbances, researchers are developing **ultra-pure metals, advanced superconductors, and specially designed insulators** that reduce unwanted interference. These materials must not only function in extreme conditions but also be manufactured with high precision, adding to the difficulty of building large-scale quantum machines.

Beyond the processors themselves, the infrastructure needed to support quantum computing is vastly different from what exists for classical computing. Today's data centers, which house thousands of traditional servers, rely on air conditioning and cooling systems to manage heat. Quantum computers, however, require specialized facilities with extreme environmental controls, including vacuum chambers, cryogenic cooling, and electromagnetic shielding to prevent outside interference.

Another major challenge is **power and energy requirements**. While quantum computing has the potential to be more energy-efficient than classical computing for certain tasks, the current infrastructure needed to maintain quantum systems is incredibly power-hungry. Cooling a single quantum processor to near absolute zero can consume as much electricity as an entire household. Scaling quantum computing to industrial levels would require new breakthroughs in energy-efficient cooling and power distribution.

Moreover, quantum computers **cannot operate in isolation**. They must connect to classical systems to process inputs, verify results, and interact with existing software. This means that alongside new materials, we also need **new types of networking and storage solutions** that can efficiently transfer information between quantum and classical systems. Developing quantum communication networks and memory storage that can preserve quantum states over long distances is a crucial step toward making quantum computing practical.

Despite these challenges, scientists and engineers around the world are making rapid progress. Research labs and technology companies are experimenting with novel materials, improving qubit stability, and developing more efficient cooling techniques. Governments and private investors are also funding large-scale projects to build the next generation of quantum infrastructure. While the road ahead is complex, overcoming these material and infrastructure challenges will be key to unlocking the full potential of quantum computing.

The challenge of making quantum computing affordable

Quantum computing has the potential to revolutionize many industries, from medicine to finance and artificial intelligence. However, for this technology to have a real impact on society, it must be accessible and affordable. Today, quantum computers are still in their early stages, and most people have never seen one, let alone used one. Unlike classical computers, which are mass-produced and widely available, quantum computers are rare, expensive, and highly specialized.

One of the biggest reasons for this is the **cost of building and maintaining a quantum computer**. Traditional computers use silicon chips, which can be manufactured efficiently and at a low cost. Quantum computers, on the other hand, require delicate qubits that are extremely sensitive to their environment. Some of these qubits, like superconducting qubits, must be kept at temperatures close to absolute zero, requiring advanced cooling systems that cost millions of dollars. Others, such as trapped ion qubits, need vacuum chambers and laser control systems, which are also expensive and complex.

The infrastructure required to operate a quantum computer adds another layer of difficulty. Quantum machines cannot simply be placed on a desk or in a regular server room like traditional computers. They require specialized laboratories with controlled environments to protect them from heat, electromagnetic radiation, and other disturbances. This makes them **inaccessible to businesses, universities, and individuals who do not have the resources to maintain such facilities**.

Even if quantum computers become more compact and easier to maintain, **the cost of development and production remains a major obstacle**. Companies and research institutions investing in quantum computing spend vast sums on research, materials, and highly specialized personnel. These costs are then reflected in the price of quantum computing services, making it difficult for small businesses, startups, and independent researchers to access this technology.

To address these issues, some companies are offering **cloud-based quantum computing services**. Instead of buying and maintaining their own quantum computers, users can access quantum processors remotely through the internet. This allows researchers and businesses to experiment with quantum computing without the need for expensive equipment. However, cloud-based access still comes with limitations, such as high costs, restricted availability, and the challenge of integrating quantum computing with classical computing systems.

Another key challenge is **making quantum computing more user-friendly**. Today, programming a quantum computer requires knowledge of quantum mechanics and specialized programming languages. This is very different from classical computing, where millions of people can write software without needing an advanced understanding of computer science. For quantum computing to become widely accessible, it must have **simpler, more intuitive software tools** that allow non-experts to take advantage of its power.

Additionally, there is a **shortage of professionals trained in quantum computing**. Because this field is still emerging, there are not enough engineers, programmers, and scientists with the necessary skills to develop and maintain quantum systems. This lack of expertise drives up costs and slows down progress. Educational institutions and companies are working to train more people in this field, but it will take time before quantum computing knowledge becomes as widespread as classical computing knowledge.

Despite these challenges, progress is being made. Advances in material science may lead to **more stable and affordable qubits**. Researchers are developing **new ways to cool quantum processors** more efficiently, reducing costs. Companies are also working on **hybrid systems** that combine classical and quantum computing, making it easier for businesses to adopt quantum solutions without completely replacing their existing infrastructure.

While quantum computing is not yet affordable for everyday use, history has shown that technology evolves rapidly. Just a few decades ago, classical computers were enormous, expensive machines that only governments and large corporations could afford. Today, we carry powerful computers in our pockets. If the same trend follows for quantum computing, what is expensive and complex today could one day become affordable and widely accessible to people around the world.

3. THE POTENTIAL OF QUANTUM COMPUTING

Why quantum computing is considered a revolution

Throughout history, technological revolutions have transformed the way we live and work. The invention of the steam engine powered the Industrial Revolution, bringing machines that could do the work of many humans. The rise of electricity gave birth to modern industry, transportation, and communication. The digital revolution, driven by classical computers, reshaped the world by making information accessible at the click of a button. Now, we stand at the beginning of a new revolution: quantum computing.

What makes quantum computing so special? The answer lies in its ability to **solve problems that are impossible for classical computers**. Traditional computers, no matter how powerful, rely on binary bits—small electronic switches that are either ON or OFF, represented as 1s and 0s. These bits process information in a linear way, meaning that even the most advanced supercomputers must go through calculations step by step.

Quantum computers work differently. Instead of binary bits, they use **quantum bits, or qubits**. These qubits can exist in multiple states at once, thanks to a property called **superposition**. Imagine flipping a coin: a classical bit is like a coin that lands either on heads or tails, while a qubit is like a coin spinning in the air, existing as both heads and tails at the same time. This allows quantum computers to process an enormous number of possibilities simultaneously.

Another key quantum property is **entanglement**, which allows qubits to be connected in such a way that changing one qubit instantly affects the other, no matter how far apart they are. This creates a level of coordination that classical computers cannot achieve, making certain types of calculations much faster.

Because of these properties, quantum computers can tackle problems that classical computers would take **millions of years** to solve. This means breakthroughs in fields such as medicine, materials science, artificial intelligence, and cybersecurity. Scientists believe quantum computing will help us **design new drugs and materials**, optimize complex systems like financial markets or transportation networks, and even create more advanced machine learning models.

One of the most talked-about applications is **cryptography**. Many of today's security systems rely on the fact that breaking encryption requires enormous amounts of computing power. Classical computers, even the most powerful ones, would need thousands of years to crack modern encryption methods. A sufficiently advanced quantum computer, however, could break these codes in minutes or hours, forcing the world to rethink cybersecurity entirely.

Beyond security, quantum computing could **transform artificial intelligence** by making machine learning algorithms far more efficient. AI models require massive amounts of data to recognize patterns and make predictions. Quantum computers could process and analyze this data much faster, leading to major advancements in healthcare, finance, and automation.

However, quantum computing is not just about speed—it is about solving problems that were previously unsolvable. For example, in **drug discovery**, researchers must analyze how molecules interact at an atomic level. Classical computers struggle to simulate these interactions accurately because they require an immense number of calculations. Quantum computers, which naturally operate under the same quantum laws as atoms and molecules, could provide **highly**

accurate simulations that speed up the development of new medicines.

In **logistics and optimization**, quantum computers could help companies plan **more efficient transportation routes, reduce energy consumption, and improve supply chains**. Airlines, shipping companies, and manufacturers all face complex problems that require testing countless possibilities to find the best solution. Quantum computing could make these decisions **much faster and more precise**, leading to massive cost savings and reduced environmental impact.

Despite these incredible possibilities, quantum computing is still in its early stages. The current machines are experimental, and practical applications are just beginning to emerge. However, history has shown that once a revolutionary technology starts gaining momentum, progress can be rapid. Just as the first classical computers were large, expensive, and difficult to use, early quantum computers are currently limited. But as research advances, these machines will become more **powerful, reliable, and accessible**.

The potential of quantum computing is **so vast that it is difficult to predict exactly how it will change our world**. What is clear, however, is that it represents a fundamental shift in computing—one that will reshape industries, accelerate scientific discovery, and unlock new possibilities that we cannot yet imagine. This is why quantum computing is not just an improvement over classical computing; it is a true revolution, one that could redefine the future of technology.

How it compares to past computing breakthroughs

Throughout history, computing has gone through several major breakthroughs that transformed the way humans process information. Each of these revolutions marked a turning point, unlocking new possibilities and reshaping industries. Quantum computing is often considered the next big leap, but to understand its significance, we need to compare it with past breakthroughs.

The birth of classical computing

Before computers, calculations were done manually or with simple mechanical devices like the abacus. In the early 20th century, machines capable of performing calculations automatically began to appear. One of the first major advances was **the invention of the transistor in 1947**, which replaced bulky vacuum tubes and allowed computers to become smaller, faster, and more reliable.

This led to the **rise of digital computing**, where information is processed using binary code—0s and 1s. Early computers were massive, filling entire rooms, yet they revolutionized industries such as banking, telecommunications, and scientific research.

The microprocessor revolution

In the 1970s, the invention of the **microprocessor** made computers smaller, cheaper, and more accessible. Instead of being limited to government agencies and large corporations, computers could now be used by businesses and individuals. This shift led to the birth of personal computers (PCs), which changed how people worked, communicated, and accessed information.

By the 1990s, the world had entered the **internet age**. With global connectivity, computers became essential tools for commerce, education, and entertainment. Data processing power increased exponentially, leading to innovations like cloud computing, artificial intelligence, and powerful mobile devices.

The rise of artificial intelligence

In recent decades, AI has pushed computing to new limits. Machine learning algorithms can now analyze massive amounts of data, recognize patterns, and even simulate human decision-making. AI powers everything from recommendation systems and facial recognition to self-driving cars and medical diagnostics.

However, even the most advanced AI models today still rely on classical computing, which has limitations. Some problems, such as simulating complex molecules for drug discovery or optimizing massive financial systems, remain too difficult or time-consuming for traditional computers to handle.

The quantum leap

Quantum computing represents an entirely new way of processing information—one that is fundamentally different from anything before. Unlike classical computers, which rely on bits that are either 0 or 1, quantum computers use **qubits**, which can exist in multiple states at once. This allows quantum computers to perform many calculations simultaneously, offering **exponential speedups** for certain types of problems.

If the transistor was the key to the digital revolution, then the qubit is the key to the quantum revolution. Just as the shift from mechanical calculators to digital computers opened the door to modern computing, the shift from classical to quantum computing could unlock entirely new capabilities that were previously impossible.

One major difference between past computing breakthroughs and quantum computing is that previous advances mostly improved **speed and efficiency**, while quantum computing introduces a **new way of thinking about computation** itself. Instead of solving problems step by step, quantum computers can explore multiple possibilities at once, making them uniquely suited for fields like cryptography, materials science, and AI.

A complement, not a replacement

It's important to note that quantum computers are not expected to replace classical computers. Just as modern AI systems still rely on classical computing hardware, quantum computers will likely work **alongside** traditional computers rather than replacing them entirely.

Think of it like this: digital calculators didn't make pen and paper obsolete, but they did make calculations much faster and easier. Similarly, quantum computers will be used for specific tasks where classical computers struggle, while everyday tasks—like browsing the internet or writing emails—will remain the domain of classical computing.

The future of computing

Looking at past breakthroughs, we see a pattern: each major shift in computing has **expanded what is possible** rather than simply replacing the previous generation of technology. Quantum computing is following the same trajectory.

While we are still in the early stages, the potential impact is enormous. Just as early computers revolutionized communication, business, and science, quantum computers could transform **medicine, finance, cybersecurity, and artificial intelligence** in ways we are only beginning to imagine.

We are standing at the edge of a new computing era—one that promises to redefine what technology can achieve. Quantum computing is not just another step forward; it is a new chapter in the story of human innovation.

The possible timeline for widespread adoption

Quantum computing is one of the most exciting technological advancements of our time. However, despite its immense potential, it is still in its early stages. Many people wonder: **When will quantum computers become a part of everyday life?** The answer is not simple, as it depends on multiple factors, including technological progress, investment, and real-world applications.

The present: the early experimental phase

At the moment, quantum computers exist, but they are far from being practical for most industries. Today's quantum computers are still in the **research and development** phase. They require highly controlled environments to function and are extremely fragile—many of them operate at temperatures close to absolute zero.

Companies like Google, IBM, and startups such as Rigetti Computing are actively working on developing better quantum systems. Some of these companies have already built quantum processors that can outperform classical computers for specific tasks. However, these breakthroughs are still mostly **experimental** and do not yet have widespread applications outside research labs.

For now, only specialized researchers and institutions have access to quantum computing, and even they are still exploring **what quantum computers can and cannot do** effectively.

The next 5 to 10 years: early industrial applications

In the coming years, we are likely to see the first practical applications of quantum computing emerge in specialized industries. Some of the early areas where quantum computers could provide value include:

- **Drug discovery and materials science:** Quantum simulations could help researchers develop new medicines and materials much faster than classical methods.

- **Optimization problems:** Industries like logistics, finance, and manufacturing could use quantum computing to optimize routes, schedules, and supply chains.

- **Artificial intelligence:** Quantum computing may enhance machine learning algorithms by providing new ways to process large amounts of data.

During this phase, quantum computers will **not yet be mainstream**. Instead, they will be used in research centers, government institutions, and large corporations that have the resources to invest in this cutting-edge technology. The general public will likely hear more about quantum computing, but they won't yet be using it in their daily lives.

The next 10 to 20 years: more widespread adoption

As technology advances, quantum computers will become more stable, powerful, and cost-effective. Researchers are working on solutions to make quantum hardware more practical, such as using error correction techniques to reduce computational mistakes.

By this stage, we can expect **some industries to fully integrate quantum computing** into their operations. Financial institutions might use quantum algorithms for risk analysis and fraud detection. Scientists might rely on quantum simulations to develop groundbreaking new materials. Even cybersecurity could change significantly, as quantum computers might be able to break today's encryption methods—leading to the rise of **quantum-resistant cryptography**.

However, everyday consumers will still not have quantum computers in their homes. Instead, companies will likely **offer quantum computing as a cloud service**, allowing businesses to access quantum power remotely, just as they use cloud computing today.

Beyond 20 Years: A Quantum Future?

Predicting what technology will look like more than 20 years from now is difficult. If quantum computing follows the path of past innovations—such as classical computing and the internet—there is a chance it could become **as common as today's personal computers and smartphones**.

For this to happen, scientists must solve some major technical challenges, including making quantum computers **more stable, affordable, and easy to use**. If these obstacles are overcome, quantum computing could become an integral part of modern technology, affecting everything from how businesses operate to how we solve global challenges like climate change and disease prevention.

A Gradual Transformation, Not an Overnight Revolution

Quantum computing will not suddenly replace classical computing. Instead, it will **gradually integrate** into different industries over the next few decades. Right now, we are at the beginning of this journey. In the next 5 to 10 years, quantum computing will remain a tool for researchers and large organizations. In 10 to 20 years, we may see **real-world commercial applications** emerge. And beyond that, quantum computing could reshape the world as we know it.

The road ahead is full of challenges, but also full of potential. The question is not **if** quantum computing will change our world—it is only a matter of **when**.

4. QUANTUM COMPUTING AND AI

How quantum computing could accelerate AI

Artificial Intelligence (AI) is already transforming the world. From virtual assistants to self-driving cars, AI helps machines learn and make decisions. However, AI still faces major challenges, especially when dealing with **huge amounts of data** and **complex problems**. Quantum computing could be the key to taking AI to the next level.

Why AI needs more computing power

Today's AI runs on classical computers, which process information using traditional bits—either a 0 or a 1. While modern supercomputers can handle large amounts of data, they struggle with **certain types of AI tasks**.

For example, training deep learning models—used in image recognition, language processing, and self-driving cars—requires **massive amounts of calculations**. The more complex the model, the more computing power is needed. Some AI models take **days, weeks, or even months** to train, even using the most powerful hardware available today.

Quantum computers, which use **qubits** instead of classical bits, could solve some of these challenges. Unlike normal bits, qubits can represent **multiple states at once**, allowing quantum computers to process information in a fundamentally different way.

How quantum computing could help AIS

One of the most promising ways quantum computing could accelerate AI is by making **machine learning** more efficient. Machine learning is the process where computers learn from data instead of being explicitly programmed. It is at the heart of many AI applications, from speech recognition to medical diagnostics.

Quantum computing could speed up machine learning in several ways:

1. **Faster Data Processing:** AI models require enormous amounts of data to learn. Quantum computers could process this data much faster than traditional computers, leading to quicker AI training times.

2. **Optimizing AI Models:** Finding the best version of an AI model often involves testing **millions of possible configurations**. Classical computers must test each option one by one. Quantum computers, however, can explore multiple possibilities at once, dramatically reducing the time needed to optimize AI algorithms.

3. **Improving Pattern Recognition:** Many AI systems, such as facial recognition or fraud detection, rely on finding patterns in data. Quantum computers could **analyze complex patterns much faster** than classical computers, improving accuracy and efficiency.

4. **Enhancing Natural Language Processing (NLP):** AI that understands human language, like chatbots or translation software, requires advanced models that analyze large texts. Quantum computing could process and interpret language data **much faster** than current methods.

Quantum AI in the real world

Several companies and research teams are already exploring the possibilities of **Quantum AI**—the combination of quantum computing and artificial intelligence.

- **Google** has tested quantum algorithms that could improve machine learning efficiency.

- **IBM** is researching how quantum computers could optimize AI applications in fields like chemistry and finance.

- **Startups** are emerging with the goal of building the first practical Quantum AI systems.

At this stage, most of this research is still experimental. Quantum computers are **not yet advanced enough** to fully replace classical AI methods. However, many scientists believe that within the next **10 to 20 years**, Quantum AI could become a major breakthrough.

The future of AI with quantum computing

The combination of quantum computing and AI could lead to a new era of intelligent machines. Imagine AI that can:

- **Develop new medicines faster** by analyzing molecules in ways classical computers cannot.

- **Predict global financial trends** with better accuracy, helping businesses make smarter decisions.

- **Create more realistic virtual assistants** that understand and respond to human emotions.

While quantum computing is still in its early stages, its potential to accelerate AI is **too big to ignore**. As researchers continue to develop more powerful quantum systems, we may one day see AI that is smarter, faster, and more capable than ever before.

The journey toward Quantum AI has just begun—but its impact could reshape the future of technology in ways we can only imagine today.

Potential breakthroughs in machine learning

Machine learning is one of the most powerful tools in modern technology. It allows computers to recognize patterns, make decisions, and even predict the future based on past data. Today, machine learning is behind many everyday applications—recommendations on streaming services, voice assistants, fraud detection, and medical diagnoses.

Despite its success, machine learning faces serious limitations. Training AI models takes enormous amounts of time and energy. Complex problems require **massive computing power**, often pushing even the most advanced computers to their limits. This is where quantum computing could make a difference.

Faster AI training

Training an AI model today can take days, weeks, or even months, depending on its complexity. The reason is simple: traditional computers can only process one calculation at a time per processor core. Even with modern supercomputers, this process remains slow.

Quantum computers, however, work differently. Thanks to **superposition**, they can process multiple possibilities at once. Instead of checking one solution at a time, a quantum computer could analyze thousands or even millions of possibilities in parallel. This could

reduce AI training time from months to hours, making machine learning much more efficient.

Improving AI's ability to learn from data

One of the biggest challenges in machine learning is analyzing vast amounts of data. Classical computers follow strict rules, meaning they struggle with uncertain or incomplete information. Quantum computers, with their ability to handle probability and uncertainty, could help AI models **make better predictions with less data**.

For example, in medical research, AI is used to analyze patient data and identify diseases. Quantum-enhanced AI could process complex genetic information much faster, helping doctors discover **new treatments and cures** more efficiently.

Solving complex optimization problems

Optimization problems exist in many industries—logistics, finance, transportation, and even weather forecasting. These problems involve finding the best solution among millions of possibilities.

Classical computers must test each option one by one, which can take an enormous amount of time. Quantum computing could **explore all possible solutions at once** and find the best one almost instantly.

Imagine an airline trying to optimize flight schedules for thousands of planes. A quantum-enhanced AI could calculate the best routes, reduce delays, and save fuel costs, making travel more efficient and environmentally friendly.

Revolutionizing natural language processing (nlp)

AI models that understand and generate human language, like chatbots and voice assistants, rely on complex language patterns. These models must process enormous datasets to learn how humans communicate.

Quantum computing could speed up this process and help AI systems **understand language more naturally**. This could lead to:

- **More advanced translation tools** that instantly translate languages with near-perfect accuracy.

- **Chatbots that understand emotions**, responding to users in a way that feels more human.

- **AI writing assistants** that generate realistic and creative text faster than ever before.

Quantum AI and Creativity

Machine learning is already used in creative fields, helping to generate art, music, and even stories. However, classical AI still struggles to **think outside the box** because it follows rigid rules.

Quantum-enhanced AI could introduce a new level of creativity. By processing multiple ideas at once and exploring **unconventional**

solutions, quantum AI could help artists, musicians, and writers create completely new forms of art.

The future of quantum machine learning

We are still in the early stages of quantum computing. Today's quantum machines are experimental, and researchers are still developing algorithms that can take full advantage of their power.

However, the potential breakthroughs in machine learning are too significant to ignore. Once quantum computing matures, it could **redefine what AI can do**—making it faster, smarter, and more powerful than ever before.

From **medical discoveries to smarter AI assistants,** quantum computing could open the door to an entirely new era of intelligent machines. The next revolution in artificial intelligence may not be decades away—it may be just around the corner.

The implications for AI research and automation

Artificial intelligence has already transformed many industries, from healthcare to finance, transportation, and entertainment. AI-powered systems help doctors detect diseases, allow self-driving cars to navigate roads, and even assist in scientific research. However, despite its impressive progress, AI still faces significant challenges. Training advanced models takes enormous time and computing power, and some problems remain too complex for even the most powerful supercomputers to handle efficiently.

Quantum computing could change this landscape dramatically. By unlocking new ways to process information, it has the potential to accelerate AI research, improve automation, and open doors to innovations that were previously thought impossible.

Faster AI model training and development

One of the biggest obstacles in AI research is the time and energy required to train complex models. Traditional computers process information in a step-by-step manner, which means that training deep learning models—especially those dealing with large amounts of data—can take weeks or even months.

Quantum computers operate differently. Instead of processing one possibility at a time, they can evaluate multiple possibilities simultaneously. This means that **AI models could be trained**

exponentially faster, reducing development time from months to days or even hours.

This breakthrough would allow researchers to test and refine AI models much more quickly, accelerating discoveries in medicine, climate science, and countless other fields. AI systems could learn more efficiently, leading to smarter and more capable algorithms.

Enhancing AI's ability to solve complex problems

Many AI-driven tasks, such as drug discovery, climate modeling, and financial forecasting, require analyzing enormous amounts of data and finding optimal solutions from countless possibilities. Classical computers often struggle with these problems because they involve too many variables and take too long to compute.

Quantum computing could **revolutionize AI's ability to tackle these challenges**. By leveraging the principles of superposition and entanglement, quantum computers can explore multiple solutions at once and find the best answers much faster.

For example, in pharmaceutical research, AI-powered quantum simulations could model molecular interactions with unmatched precision. This could lead to **faster drug discovery**, reducing the time it takes to develop life-saving treatments. Similarly, AI-enhanced by quantum computing could improve climate predictions, optimize energy consumption, and create more effective strategies for managing resources.

Smarter automation and decision-making

Automation is becoming an essential part of industries worldwide, from manufacturing to finance and logistics. AI-driven automation systems analyze vast amounts of data to make real-time decisions, but they are limited by the computing power of traditional systems.

Quantum-enhanced AI could take automation to a new level. By processing data more efficiently and handling uncertainty better, quantum-powered AI systems could:

- **Improve financial market predictions**, allowing banks and investors to make better decisions.

- **Enhance supply chain management**, optimizing global logistics networks to reduce waste and increase efficiency.

- **Advance autonomous vehicles**, enabling self-driving cars to react more quickly and safely in complex environments.

In robotics, quantum AI could make machines **far more adaptable and responsive**, allowing them to handle more complex tasks with greater precision. Factories, for instance, could deploy **highly intelligent robotic systems** capable of making real-time adjustments to optimize production.

Ethical and security considerations

With great power comes great responsibility. The combination of quantum computing and AI raises important questions about security, ethics, and control. If AI becomes significantly more powerful, how do we ensure it remains safe and aligned with human values?

One concern is cybersecurity. Quantum computers will eventually be able to break many of today's encryption methods, making current security systems obsolete. This could create risks if AI-driven automation systems fall into the wrong hands.

Another concern is decision-making transparency. AI models today can be difficult to interpret, but adding quantum computing could make them even more complex. Ensuring that AI systems remain explainable and accountable will be crucial.

The future of AI and quantum computing

While quantum computing is still in its early stages, the potential it holds for AI research and automation is immense. Over the coming decades, we could see:

- AI models that **learn faster and make better predictions**.

- Automation systems that **solve problems previously thought impossible**.

- New discoveries in science, medicine, and engineering driven by **quantum-enhanced AI**.

As these technologies continue to evolve, researchers, policymakers, and businesses will need to work together to harness their power responsibly. If developed with care, the fusion of quantum computing and artificial intelligence could **reshape the future**, bringing solutions to some of the world's most pressing challenges.

5. QUANTUM COMPUTING AND CYBERSECURITY

The rise of quantum computing brings both exciting possibilities and serious concerns, especially in the field of cybersecurity. While traditional computers rely on complex mathematical problems to keep data safe, quantum computers could one day solve these problems much faster, potentially breaking the encryption systems we depend on today.

This shift has led researchers and governments to prepare for a future where current security methods may no longer be reliable. New encryption techniques are being developed to counteract these risks, ensuring that sensitive information remains protected even in a world where quantum computers exist.

Beyond encryption, quantum computing could reshape the way data is handled, stored, and analyzed. It could offer stronger security solutions but also raise new challenges related to privacy and surveillance. As this technology evolves, it will be crucial to strike a balance between innovation and protection, ensuring that quantum computing enhances security rather than weakening it.

The risk to current encryption methods

Encryption is the foundation of digital security. Every time you send a message, make an online purchase, or access your bank account, encryption ensures that your data remains private. Modern encryption techniques rely on complex mathematical problems that traditional computers would take thousands—or even millions—of years to solve. This makes them practically unbreakable. However, quantum computing threatens to change this reality.

At the heart of the issue is how quantum computers process information. Unlike classical computers, which work with bits (0s and 1s), quantum computers use **qubits**, which can exist in multiple states at once. This allows them to perform many calculations simultaneously. A special quantum algorithm, known as **Shor's algorithm**, could one day be used to break the most common encryption methods in minutes or even seconds.

One of the biggest concerns is the security of the **RSA encryption system**, which protects everything from emails to financial transactions. RSA is based on the difficulty of factoring large numbers—a problem that is practically impossible for classical computers to solve efficiently. But a powerful enough quantum computer could break RSA encryption quickly, exposing sensitive data to hackers, governments, or any entity with access to quantum technology.

The potential impact is enormous. If encryption methods become obsolete, confidential communications, personal data, and even national security secrets could be at risk. The transition to new security standards is not simple. Large institutions, from banks to government agencies, will need to upgrade their systems to resist quantum attacks. This has led to the rise of **post-quantum cryptography**, which focuses on developing encryption techniques that even quantum computers cannot break.

Despite the risks, quantum computing is still in its early stages. Current quantum machines are not yet powerful enough to break encryption. However, experts warn that it is only a matter of time before they become strong enough to pose a real threat. This is why researchers, governments, and private companies are racing to develop new security measures before quantum computing reaches its full potential.

For now, encryption remains secure, but the countdown has already begun. The challenge is clear: the world must prepare for the quantum era before it arrives.

Post-quantum cryptography

Healthcare is undergoing a seismic shift, with AI at the forefront of advancements in diagnostics, treatment planning, and patient care. AI-powered diagnostic tools analyze medical images, such as X-rays and MRIs, with remarkable precision, often matching or surpassing human radiologists. For instance, AI algorithms have been instrumental in early detection of diseases like cancer, improving survival rates by enabling timely intervention.

In treatment planning, AI helps tailor therapies to individual patients. By analyzing genetic data and medical histories, AI systems recommend personalized treatment regimens, ensuring higher success rates and fewer side effects. Additionally, AI-powered robots assist in surgeries, enhancing precision and reducing recovery times.

AI's role in administrative tasks cannot be overlooked. Automated systems streamline patient scheduling, manage electronic health records, and handle billing, freeing up healthcare professionals to focus on patient care. Telemedicine platforms, powered by AI, also gained prominence during the COVID-19 pandemic, providing remote consultations and expanding access to healthcare in underserved regions.

The balance between privacy and surveillance

In agriculture, AI is fostering a new era of precision farming. Farmers use AI-driven tools to monitor crop health, predict weather patterns, and optimize irrigation systems. These technologies not only enhance productivity but also promote sustainable practices.

For example, drones equipped with AI-powered cameras scan fields, identifying areas affected by pests or diseases. This targeted approach allows farmers to apply treatments only where needed, reducing costs and minimizing environmental impact. Similarly, AI models analyze soil conditions and recommend the optimal mix of fertilizers, ensuring maximum yield without overuse of chemicals.

AI is also transforming supply chain management in agriculture. By predicting demand and monitoring logistics, AI systems ensure that produce reaches markets in the shortest time possible, reducing food waste and increasing profitability.

6. KEY APPLICATIONS OF QUANTUM COMPUTING

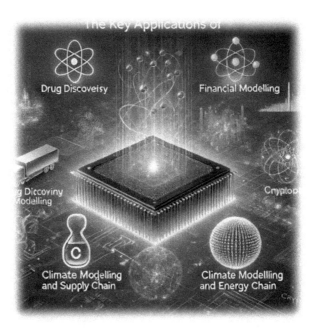

Quantum computing is not just a theoretical concept—it has the potential to revolutionize many industries. While traditional computers are excellent for most everyday tasks, they struggle with certain types of complex problems that require enormous amounts of processing power. Quantum computers, with their unique ability to handle multiple possibilities at once, could solve problems that would take classical computers centuries to process.

From medicine to finance, logistics to artificial intelligence, quantum computing could bring breakthroughs that were once thought impossible. Scientists hope to develop life-saving drugs faster, optimize supply chains more efficiently, and even create more advanced AI systems. Though quantum computers are still in their early stages, researchers and companies around the world are exploring how this technology could reshape the future.

In this chapter, we will explore the key areas where quantum computing could have the greatest impact. These applications will not only transform industries but could also change the way we live and work.

Drug discovery and medical research

The search for new medicines is a long and complex process. It often takes years, even decades, to develop a single drug. Scientists must test millions of chemical compounds to see which ones might work against a disease. Even with the help of powerful computers, this process is slow because traditional computers can only analyze one possibility at a time.

Quantum computing could change this completely. Unlike classical computers, quantum computers can explore many possible solutions at once. This means they could quickly identify promising drug candidates, reducing the time needed for research and development. Scientists hope that quantum computing will help them design new treatments for diseases such as cancer, Alzheimer's, and rare genetic disorders much faster than today's methods allow.

Another exciting possibility is the ability to model complex biological molecules. Proteins, for example, are difficult to understand because they fold into incredibly complicated shapes. The way a protein folds determines how it functions in the human body, and mistakes in folding can cause serious diseases. Quantum computers could simulate protein folding with much greater accuracy than classical computers, helping researchers discover new treatments and even prevent diseases before they develop.

Beyond drug discovery, quantum computing could also improve personalized medicine. Today, treatments are often designed to work for most people, but they don't always consider individual differences in genetics and biology. With quantum computing, doctors could analyze a person's unique genetic makeup and design treatments tailored specifically to them. This could lead to more effective therapies with fewer side effects.

The potential of quantum computing in medicine is enormous. While the technology is still developing, researchers around the world are already working on ways to use it for solving some of the biggest medical challenges. If successful, quantum computing could lead to medical breakthroughs that save millions of lives and improve healthcare for everyone.

Financial modeling and economic predictions

The financial world is full of uncertainty. Investors, banks, and governments constantly try to predict how markets will behave, how risks will evolve, and how economic policies will affect growth. However, financial systems are incredibly complex, involving thousands of factors that interact in unpredictable ways. Traditional computers, even the most powerful ones, struggle to process this vast amount of data efficiently.

Quantum computing offers a new approach to solving financial problems. Unlike classical computers, which analyze one possibility at a time, quantum computers can explore many potential outcomes simultaneously. This could make financial models much more accurate, helping businesses and policymakers make better decisions.

One of the biggest challenges in finance is risk management. Companies and investors need to predict potential losses due to changes in market conditions, interest rates, or unexpected events. Quantum computers could process vast amounts of financial data and simulate different scenarios much faster than today's computers. This would allow firms to prepare for market crashes, inflation changes, or economic downturns with much greater precision.

Portfolio optimization is another area that could benefit from quantum computing. Investors aim to build portfolios that balance risk and reward, selecting the best combination of assets to maximize returns. Today's methods rely on complex mathematical models that require enormous computing power. Quantum computers could perform these calculations in seconds, making it easier for investors to create highly optimized portfolios.

In economic predictions, governments and institutions analyze global trends to forecast economic growth, unemployment rates, and inflation. These predictions require processing massive datasets and identifying patterns that influence economies. Quantum computing could improve economic forecasting models, helping governments respond faster to economic crises and make more informed policy decisions.

Fraud detection is another critical area where quantum computing could have a major impact. Financial institutions constantly monitor transactions to detect suspicious activities, such as credit card fraud or money laundering. Quantum computers could analyze transaction patterns in real time, identifying fraudulent activities more accurately and reducing financial crime.

While quantum computing is still in its early stages, financial institutions and banks are already exploring its potential. If successful, quantum-powered financial models could revolutionize the way we understand and manage money, leading to a more stable and efficient global economy.

Logistics and supply chain optimization

Every product we use—whether it's food, clothing, or electronics—must travel through a complex network before reaching us. This network, known as the supply chain, includes manufacturers, warehouses, transportation systems, and retail stores. Managing this network efficiently is crucial for businesses and consumers alike. However, optimizing supply chains is an extremely difficult task, involving millions of variables such as traffic conditions, delivery times, fuel costs, and storage capacities.

Traditional computers already help companies manage logistics, but they have limitations. As supply chains grow larger and more complex, finding the best routes, schedules, and resource allocations becomes increasingly difficult. This is where quantum computing could make a significant difference.

Quantum computers can process vast amounts of data and explore multiple solutions at the same time. This ability allows them to quickly identify the most efficient ways to transport goods, reduce delivery times, and minimize costs. For example, a quantum computer could analyze weather forecasts, road conditions, and fuel prices simultaneously to determine the fastest and cheapest route for a shipment.

One of the biggest challenges in logistics is demand prediction. Businesses need to know how much stock to produce and where to send it before customers even place their orders. If they produce too much, they waste money. If they produce too little, they lose sales. Quantum computing could improve demand forecasting by analyzing historical sales data, economic trends, and even social media activity to predict future demand with greater accuracy.

Another major issue is warehouse management. Large companies store products in multiple locations and must decide which items should be kept where. Quantum computers could help optimize warehouse layouts, ensuring that goods are stored in the most accessible places and reducing the time needed to process orders.

Airports, shipping companies, and delivery services also face enormous logistical challenges. A company like FedEx or Amazon, which handles millions of packages daily, must constantly adjust its delivery routes in real time. Quantum computing could process these adjustments instantly, allowing for more efficient operations and reducing costs.

As businesses continue to expand globally, supply chains will become even more complex. Quantum computing has the potential to transform logistics by making supply chains faster, more cost-effective, and more adaptable to sudden changes. This could lead to lower prices for consumers, fewer delays, and a more sustainable approach to global trade.

Climate modeling and energy efficiency

Understanding and predicting the Earth's climate is one of the most complex scientific challenges of our time. Climate models rely on vast amounts of data, including atmospheric conditions, ocean currents, greenhouse gas levels, and solar activity. Traditional computers have made significant progress in climate modeling, but they still struggle to process the enormous number of variables involved. This is where quantum computing could revolutionize the field.

Quantum computers have the ability to analyze massive datasets and simulate complex systems much faster than classical computers. This could lead to more accurate climate predictions, helping scientists understand how different factors influence global warming and extreme weather events. With better models, governments and organizations could develop more effective strategies to mitigate climate change and prepare for natural disasters.

One major challenge in climate science is predicting long-term changes with high precision. Today's models require simplifications to make calculations feasible, often leading to uncertainties in forecasts. Quantum computing could improve these models by processing more data simultaneously and considering interactions between countless environmental factors. This could provide a clearer picture of how the climate will evolve over decades or even centuries.

In addition to climate modeling, quantum computing could play a crucial role in energy efficiency. The global demand for energy continues to rise, and optimizing energy consumption is essential for both economic and environmental reasons. Quantum algorithms could help design smarter energy grids that distribute electricity more efficiently, reducing waste and lowering costs.

Renewable energy sources, such as wind and solar power, are vital for reducing dependence on fossil fuels. However, managing these energy sources is complex because they depend on weather conditions that constantly change. Quantum computers could help optimize the integration of renewable energy into power grids by predicting fluctuations in energy production and adjusting distribution accordingly.

Another exciting application is the development of better battery technologies. Quantum computing could accelerate the discovery of new materials for batteries, leading to longer-lasting and more efficient energy storage solutions. This would have a significant impact on electric vehicles and renewable energy storage, making clean energy more accessible and reliable.

The potential of quantum computing in climate science and energy efficiency is enormous. By improving our ability to predict climate patterns and optimize energy use, it could contribute to a more sustainable future. While these technologies are still in their early stages, their impact could be life-changing for future generations.

7. QUANTUM COMPUTING AND SCIENCE

Science has always advanced through better tools, from the telescope that revealed distant galaxies to the microscope that uncovered the world of cells. Quantum computing is one of the next great tools, offering new ways to solve problems that were previously impossible or took too long for classical computers to handle.

In fields like physics, chemistry, and biology, quantum computers could lead to breakthroughs by simulating complex systems with incredible precision. Scientists could explore the mysteries of the universe, design new materials, and even unlock secrets hidden in

DNA. By harnessing the strange properties of quantum mechanics, these machines have the potential to push the boundaries of human knowledge in ways we are only beginning to imagine.

Advancing physics and chemistry through simulations

Quantum computing has the potential to revolutionize physics and chemistry by allowing scientists to simulate complex systems that are currently beyond the reach of classical computers. Traditional computers struggle to accurately model the behavior of atoms and molecules because they rely on binary logic, which simplifies reality into ones and zeros. However, quantum computers operate using quantum bits (qubits), which can represent multiple states at once. This unique capability allows them to process vast amounts of data simultaneously, making it possible to simulate the behavior of matter at the atomic and subatomic levels with unprecedented accuracy.

In physics, quantum computers could help researchers explore the mysteries of the universe. For example, they could simulate the behavior of particles at extreme conditions, such as inside black holes or during the first moments after the Big Bang. These simulations could provide new insights into the fundamental laws of nature, including how gravity interacts with quantum mechanics—one of the biggest unsolved questions in modern physics.

In chemistry, the ability to simulate molecular interactions with high precision could lead to groundbreaking discoveries. One of the most promising applications is in the design of new materials with extraordinary properties. Scientists could create superconductors that conduct electricity without resistance, leading to more efficient power grids and advanced electronics. They could also develop stronger, lighter materials for construction, aerospace, and medicine.

Another major impact of quantum computing in chemistry is in drug discovery. Many life-saving medicines are created by designing molecules that interact with the human body in specific ways. Quantum simulations could help predict how different molecules will behave before they are tested in laboratories, significantly speeding up the drug development process. This could lead to faster cures for diseases, more effective treatments, and fewer side effects.

By giving scientists the power to simulate nature at an unprecedented level, quantum computing is opening doors to new discoveries that could change our understanding of the physical world and improve many aspects of daily life.

Health and life expansion

For centuries, humanity has sought ways to combat disease and extend life. Traditional medicine and modern computing have already made extraordinary progress, but there are still many challenges that classical computers cannot solve fast enough. Quantum computing has the potential to revolutionize healthcare by unlocking new ways to diagnose, treat, and even prevent diseases.

One of the greatest strengths of quantum computers is their ability to process vast amounts of data simultaneously. Unlike classical computers, which analyze one possibility at a time, quantum computers can explore multiple solutions at once. This capability is particularly important for understanding complex biological systems, such as how diseases develop and spread in the human body.

Take, for example, drug discovery. Developing new medicines is a slow and expensive process. Researchers must test thousands of chemical compounds to find one that effectively treats a disease. Quantum computers could simulate molecular interactions at an unprecedented speed, allowing scientists to predict which drugs will work best before conducting physical experiments. This could significantly reduce the time needed to create new treatments, potentially leading to faster cures for diseases like cancer, Alzheimer's, and Parkinson's.

Another promising area is personalized medicine. Every person's body is unique, meaning that some treatments work well for one individual but fail for another. With quantum computing, doctors could analyze a patient's genetic information in a fraction of the time it takes today. By understanding a person's genetic makeup, doctors could design treatments tailored to their specific needs, reducing side effects and improving the effectiveness of therapies.

Quantum computing could also revolutionize the fight against infectious diseases. When a new virus emerges, scientists race against time to understand its structure and develop vaccines. Quantum simulations could predict how a virus mutates, enabling researchers to create vaccines before the virus spreads widely. This could prevent pandemics and save millions of lives.

In addition to treating diseases, quantum computing may help scientists unlock the secrets of aging itself. Aging is a complex process influenced by genetic, environmental, and biochemical factors. By analyzing these interactions on a quantum level, researchers may discover ways to slow down aging, repair damaged cells, and extend human life. While the idea of dramatically increasing human lifespan may still seem like science fiction, quantum-powered research is bringing us closer to a future where people live longer, healthier lives.

Quantum computing is not a magical solution that will eliminate all diseases overnight. Many challenges remain, such as building stable quantum systems and developing algorithms that can effectively process biological data. However, the potential is undeniable. With continued research and investment, quantum computing may soon redefine medicine, making diseases that were once incurable a thing of the past.

As we stand at the edge of this new era, one thing is clear: quantum computing is not just about making computers faster. It is about saving lives, improving health, and giving humanity the tools to overcome its greatest biological challenges.

Solving the problem of energy production with nuclear fusion

Energy is the foundation of modern civilization. Every machine, home, and city rely on a continuous supply of power. Today, most of our energy comes from fossil fuels, which are limited and polluting, or from renewable sources, which depend on natural conditions like wind and sunlight. Scientists have long searched for a perfect energy source—one that is clean, unlimited, and reliable. This search has led to one of the most exciting scientific challenges of our time: nuclear fusion.

Nuclear fusion is the process that powers the sun and stars. It happens when atoms are forced together under extreme heat and pressure, releasing massive amounts of energy. Unlike nuclear fission, which is used in today's power plants and creates dangerous radioactive waste, fusion produces only a small amount of harmless helium as a byproduct. It also does not carry the risk of catastrophic meltdowns. If we can successfully harness fusion on Earth, it could provide nearly limitless energy with no greenhouse gas emissions.

The problem, however, is that fusion requires incredibly high temperatures—millions of degrees—before atoms can merge. Creating and maintaining these extreme conditions has been one of the biggest challenges in science and engineering. This is where quantum computing could change the game.

Traditional computers, even the most powerful supercomputers, struggle to accurately simulate the complex physics of nuclear fusion. The interactions between particles happen at an atomic level, where quantum mechanics rules. Quantum computers, which process information in a fundamentally different way than classical computers, are much better suited for these kinds of calculations. They can model atomic behavior with far greater precision, helping scientists understand and control fusion reactions more efficiently.

With quantum computing, researchers can simulate how different materials behave under fusion conditions, predict the best ways to contain plasma (the superheated state of matter needed for fusion), and optimize reactor designs. These insights could dramatically accelerate progress toward a working fusion reactor.

In space, fusion could be the key to solving one of humanity's biggest challenges: how to power long-term missions to other planets. Current spacecraft rely on chemical fuels or solar power, both of which have limitations. A compact fusion reactor could provide a nearly endless energy supply for deep-space exploration, making it possible to travel farther than ever before. It could also support human settlements on the Moon or Mars, providing constant power even in environments where solar energy is unreliable.

The race to achieve practical nuclear fusion is already underway, with major research projects around the world working toward the first functional reactors. While challenges remain, the combination of quantum computing and fusion research is opening up possibilities that once seemed like science fiction. If successful, this breakthrough could redefine the future of energy on Earth and beyond, making clean and abundant power available for all.

Understanding the universe at a deeper level

The universe is full of mysteries, from the nature of black holes to the origins of space and time. Scientists have spent centuries trying to unlock its secrets using mathematics, physics, and powerful computers. However, some questions are so complex that even the most advanced supercomputers struggle to provide answers. This is where quantum computing could make a difference.

Quantum computers have the potential to process information in a way that mimics the behavior of the universe itself. Unlike traditional computers, which use binary digits (ones and zeros) to perform calculations, quantum computers use qubits, which can exist in multiple states at once. This allows them to explore vast possibilities simultaneously, making them incredibly powerful tools for scientific discovery.

One of the most exciting possibilities is the study of **quantum mechanics**, the branch of physics that describes how particles behave at the smallest scales. At the quantum level, particles can exist in multiple places at once, teleport across space, and even influence each other instantly, regardless of distance. Understanding these strange behaviors could help scientists develop new theories that explain the fundamental nature of reality.

Quantum computing could also help us explore the **origins of the universe**. Many scientists believe that the universe began with the Big Bang, a massive explosion that created space, time, and matter. However, what happened in the very first moments remains a mystery. By simulating the extreme conditions of the early universe, quantum computers could help us understand how galaxies, stars, and planets formed.

Another important area of research is **black holes**, which are regions of space where gravity is so strong that nothing, not even light, can escape. Black holes challenge our understanding of physics, especially when it comes to how information behaves at their edges. Quantum computing could help scientists develop better models to explain how black holes form, how they interact with their surroundings, and what happens inside them.

Beyond black holes and the Big Bang, quantum computers could also help answer one of the biggest questions in science: **What is dark matter and dark energy?** These invisible forces make up most of the universe, yet we know very little about them. Scientists believe dark matter holds galaxies together, while dark energy drives the universe's expansion. However, since these forces do not emit light, they are extremely difficult to study. Quantum simulations could allow scientists to test new theories and possibly discover what these mysterious forces really are.

By providing a deeper understanding of the universe, quantum computing could lead to new breakthroughs in physics, cosmology, and space exploration. It could help answer questions that humans have been asking for centuries and open new frontiers in our knowledge of reality itself.

Tyler Soloway

The role of quantum computing in fundamental research

Quantum computing is more than just a tool for faster problem-solving in business and technology; it is a groundbreaking approach that can deepen our understanding of nature itself. At the heart of fundamental research is the quest to explain how matter and energy interact at the smallest scales, and traditional computers often struggle with the immense complexity of these systems. Quantum computers, using qubits that can exist in multiple states simultaneously, naturally mimic the behavior of particles, allowing scientists to simulate and study phenomena with unprecedented accuracy.

By accurately modeling the interactions of atoms, molecules, and even subatomic particles, quantum computing offers researchers a window into the basic laws of physics. This ability is crucial for exploring challenging areas such as high-energy physics, where experiments require vast computational resources and yield data that classical methods can only approximate. Quantum simulations can help test theories about the forces that govern the universe, shedding light on topics from superconductivity to the very origins of space and time.

Furthermore, quantum computing holds promise for unifying concepts in physics that have long remained separate, such as the ideas behind quantum mechanics and general relativity. This unification is one of the most profound challenges in science today, and the unique power of quantum systems may provide the necessary insights to bridge these

92

theories. Additionally, quantum models of chemical reactions offer the potential to transform our understanding of complex processes in nature, leading to breakthroughs in areas like energy storage and drug development.

In essence, quantum computing serves as a new lens through which scientists can observe and interpret the fundamental workings of the universe. As the technology continues to advance, its contributions to fundamental research will likely reveal answers to some of the most enduring mysteries in science, opening up new pathways to knowledge and innovation.

8. QUANTUM COMPUTING AND SPACE EXPLORATION

Space is vast, mysterious, and filled with challenges that push the limits of human knowledge. As we strive to explore the universe, traditional computers often struggle with the enormous amounts of data and complex calculations required for space missions. Quantum computing offers a new way to tackle these challenges by processing information in ways that classical computers cannot.

From plotting the most efficient routes for interplanetary travel to analyzing deep-space signals, quantum computing has the potential to revolutionize space exploration. By solving problems faster and more accurately, it could help scientists uncover new planets, understand the nature of black holes, and even search for signs of life beyond Earth. As this technology advances, it may become a key tool in humanity's quest to explore the final frontier.

Solving complex space travel challenges

Space travel is one of the most difficult challenges humanity has ever faced. Sending astronauts or robotic probes to distant planets requires solving an incredible number of problems, from planning the best route through space to ensuring that spacecraft have enough fuel and supplies for the journey. Traditional computers have helped scientists design missions, but they struggle with the enormous complexity of space travel. This is where quantum computing could make a real difference.

One of the biggest challenges in space travel is navigation. Spacecraft must travel millions or even billions of kilometers across the solar system, avoiding obstacles like asteroids and making precise course corrections along the way. Quantum computers can process vast amounts of data quickly and find the most efficient routes, reducing travel time and saving resources. This could be especially useful for planning missions to Mars and beyond.

Another major challenge is communication. The farther a spacecraft travels from Earth, the longer it takes for signals to reach mission control. Quantum computing could improve the way data is transmitted and processed, making space communication faster and more reliable. Scientists are even exploring the idea of quantum teleportation, which could one day allow instant communication over vast distances.

Space missions also involve extreme conditions. Astronauts face dangers such as radiation exposure, equipment failures, and unexpected space weather events. Quantum computing could help by simulating these risks in detail, allowing scientists to prepare for different scenarios before launching a mission. This could lead to better spacecraft designs and safer space travel.

Additionally, quantum computing could play a key role in managing resources during long-duration missions. Whether it's optimizing the use of energy, recycling air and water, or managing food supplies, quantum algorithms could help ensure that astronauts have everything they need to survive in deep space.

As we look toward the future, quantum computing may be the key to solving many of the challenges that stand between us and interplanetary travel. It has the potential to make space missions more efficient, safer, and even open new possibilities for exploring distant worlds.

Optimizing spacecraft design and mission planning

Designing a spacecraft is one of the most complex engineering tasks in the world. Every component, from the fuel system to the communication antennas, must be carefully planned to ensure the mission's success. Traditional computers can help, but as missions become more ambitious—such as sending humans to Mars or exploring distant moons—more advanced tools are needed. This is where quantum computing could play a revolutionary role.

One of the biggest challenges in spacecraft design is balancing weight, efficiency, and durability. Every kilogram launched into space is costly, so engineers must make sure that the spacecraft is as light as possible while still being strong enough to survive extreme conditions. Quantum computers can analyze millions of possible designs and materials far more quickly than traditional computers, helping engineers find the best solutions in a fraction of the time.

Mission planning is another area where quantum computing could bring significant improvements. Before launching a spacecraft, scientists must consider thousands of factors: the best launch window, the safest route through space, how much fuel is needed, and how to maximize energy from solar panels. Each of these decisions requires complex calculations, which can take months or even years using classical computers. Quantum algorithms can speed up this process by rapidly evaluating multiple scenarios at once, allowing space agencies to develop more efficient and cost-effective missions.

For long-duration missions, such as sending astronauts to Mars, planning becomes even more complicated. A small mistake in calculations could mean running out of oxygen, food, or energy before reaching the destination. Quantum computing could help predict and prevent such problems by simulating different mission conditions in great detail. It could optimize supply chains, ensure backup systems are in place, and even suggest alternative plans in case something goes wrong.

Beyond just planning, quantum computing could also help spacecraft navigate better once they are in space. By analyzing gravitational forces, space weather, and the positions of celestial bodies, quantum algorithms could make real-time adjustments to a spacecraft's trajectory, improving precision and safety. This could be especially useful for landings on planets or asteroids, where the slightest miscalculation could lead to a crash.

As space exploration continues to push the boundaries of what is possible, quantum computing will become an essential tool for designing better spacecraft and planning smarter missions. It has the potential to make space travel more efficient, safer, and ultimately help humanity reach farther than ever before.

The potential for deep-space communication and navigation

As space exploration reaches farther into the universe, communication and navigation become increasingly difficult. Traditional radio signals, which have been used to communicate with spacecraft for decades, take longer to travel as missions move deeper into space. For example, a message sent from Earth to Mars can take up to 20 minutes to arrive, and signals sent to even more distant destinations, like Jupiter or Saturn, can take over an hour. This delay makes real-time communication and navigation nearly impossible. Quantum computing offers a potential breakthrough by helping develop faster, more reliable ways to connect with spacecraft and guide them through the vastness of space.

One of the most promising possibilities is the use of quantum mechanics in communication. Scientists are exploring a concept called **quantum entanglement**, where two particles become linked in such a way that changes in one instantaneously affect the other, no matter how far apart they are. If this principle could be applied to deep-space communication, it could allow near-instantaneous data transmission between Earth and distant spacecraft. While this technology is still in its early stages, quantum computing could help process and manage the vast amount of data required to make quantum communication a reality.

Quantum computers could also play a key role in enhancing traditional communication methods. Spacecraft send and receive huge amounts of data, including images, sensor readings, and navigation updates. However, these signals weaken as they travel through space, making them difficult to interpret when they reach Earth. Quantum algorithms could improve how signals are processed, reducing errors and allowing clearer, faster communication over extreme distances. This could be especially useful for missions exploring the outer planets or even interstellar space.

Navigation is another critical challenge for deep-space missions. In the absence of GPS satellites, which only work around Earth, spacecraft rely on tracking signals from Earth-based stations. However, this method becomes less effective as spacecraft travel farther away. Quantum computing could improve space navigation by processing vast amounts of astronomical data to help spacecraft determine their exact position more accurately.

One possible application is **quantum clocks**, which are far more precise than any existing timekeeping technology. Spacecraft equipped with quantum clocks could navigate independently, reducing their reliance on Earth-based signals. This would be especially useful for crewed missions to Mars or beyond, where astronauts will need to operate autonomously without waiting for instructions from Earth.

Beyond our solar system, quantum computing could help in planning missions to explore exoplanets—planets orbiting other stars. By analyzing gravitational fields, radiation levels, and possible hazards, quantum algorithms could calculate the safest and most efficient routes for future interstellar spacecraft.

As humanity ventures farther into space, the challenges of communication and navigation will grow. Quantum computing has the potential to revolutionize these areas, making deep-space travel more efficient, reliable, and perhaps even allowing instant communication across the cosmos. While many of these ideas are still in development, quantum computing may one day be the key to unlocking the next era of space exploration.

9. QUANTUM COMPUTING AND BUSINESS

Technology has always shaped the way businesses operate, from the invention of the printing press to the rise of the internet. Now, quantum computing promises to be the next major revolution. While traditional computers struggle with certain complex problems, quantum computers have the potential to solve them much faster, unlocking new possibilities in finance, logistics, healthcare, and many other industries.

Companies are beginning to explore how quantum computing can optimize supply chains, improve financial forecasting, and even revolutionize cybersecurity. Although this technology is still in its early stages, businesses that understand its potential today will be better prepared for the future. In this chapter, we will explore how quantum computing could transform the world of business and change the way companies make decisions, process data, and innovate.

How industries will leverage quantum computing

Quantum computing has the potential to change industries in ways that were once unimaginable. Unlike traditional computers, which process information in a linear way, quantum computers can explore multiple possibilities at the same time. This could help businesses solve problems that are too complex for today's most powerful supercomputers.

One of the first industries to benefit will be **finance**. Banks and investment firms could use quantum computers to improve risk analysis, detect fraud more accurately, and develop better financial models. With their ability to process vast amounts of data instantly, quantum computers could help institutions predict market movements with greater precision.

In **healthcare**, quantum computing could accelerate drug discovery by simulating how molecules interact at the quantum level. This could lead to the development of new medicines in a fraction of the time it takes today. Hospitals and research labs could also use quantum algorithms to analyze genetic data, leading to more personalized treatments for patients.

The **logistics and transportation** industry could optimize routes and schedules in ways never before possible. Airlines, shipping companies, and delivery services deal with incredibly complex problems, such as minimizing delays while reducing fuel consumption. A quantum computer could analyze millions of potential routes at once, helping businesses save time and money while reducing their environmental impact.

Cybersecurity will also undergo a transformation. While quantum computing poses a threat to traditional encryption methods, it also offers new solutions. Businesses will be able to develop ultra-secure encryption techniques based on quantum principles, making sensitive data nearly impossible to hack.

Manufacturing and engineering will see advancements through **materials science**. Quantum computers could help design stronger and lighter materials, improving everything from airplane construction to consumer electronics. This could lead to more durable products, lower production costs, and reduced waste.

Even the **energy sector** could benefit. Quantum computing could help optimize power grids, making electricity distribution more efficient. It could also accelerate research into new energy sources, such as advanced batteries or nuclear fusion.

While quantum computing is still in its early stages, industries are already preparing for its arrival. Companies that embrace this technology early will have a competitive advantage, unlocking new possibilities that were previously out of reach. Quantum computing will not replace traditional computers, but it will become a powerful tool for solving some of the world's most difficult problems, shaping the future of business in the process.

The impact on banking, insurance, and financial markets

Quantum computing has the potential to revolutionize the world of finance. Banks, insurance companies, and financial markets rely on massive amounts of data and complex calculations to make decisions. Today's computers do an excellent job, but they still have limits. Quantum computers, with their ability to process information in entirely new ways, could bring game-changing improvements in risk management, fraud detection, portfolio optimization, and financial modeling.

One of the biggest challenges in banking is managing **risk**. Financial institutions must assess the likelihood of loans being repaid, the stability of markets, and potential losses in investments. Traditional risk models rely on historical data and statistical methods, but they are not perfect. Quantum computers could analyze far more variables at once, creating more accurate predictions about market movements and economic trends. This could help banks make better decisions and reduce financial crises.

Insurance companies also depend heavily on risk calculations. When determining the cost of an insurance policy, they must evaluate multiple factors—health history, climate risks, accident probabilities, and economic conditions. Quantum computing could improve these calculations, allowing insurers to offer more personalized policies while minimizing financial losses. Customers could benefit from fairer pricing based on a deeper understanding of risk factors.

Another area where quantum computing could make a major impact is **fraud detection**. Financial fraud is a global problem, costing businesses billions of dollars each year. Current fraud detection systems rely on pattern recognition, but criminals are constantly finding new ways to bypass security measures. Quantum computers could analyze transactions in real time, detecting suspicious activity faster and more accurately than ever before. This could make banking systems safer and protect customers from financial crime.

In investment and trading, quantum computing could change the way financial markets operate. Traders rely on complex algorithms to analyze data and predict price movements. However, the stock market is influenced by countless factors, making it difficult to predict accurately. Quantum computers could process vast amounts of financial data instantly, identifying hidden patterns that traditional computers might miss. This could lead to better investment strategies and more stable markets.

Cryptography, which is essential for secure transactions, could also be transformed. Today's encryption methods are based on mathematical problems that are difficult for classical computers to solve. However, quantum computers could break some of these encryption systems, forcing banks and businesses to develop new security measures. At the same time, quantum-based encryption methods are emerging, promising an even higher level of security in financial transactions.

The impact of quantum computing on finance will not happen overnight. The technology is still developing, and it may take years before it becomes widely used. However, banks, insurance companies, and financial institutions are already investing in research to prepare for the future. Those that adapt early could gain a major advantage, unlocking new ways to manage risk, detect fraud, and optimize financial operations.

In the long run, quantum computing has the potential to make financial systems smarter, safer, and more efficient. It may not replace traditional computing entirely, but it will become a powerful tool, reshaping the way businesses in the financial sector operate.

Optimization of Financial Markets

Financial markets operate on vast amounts of data, with traders, institutions, and investors constantly seeking ways to gain an edge. Traditional computing has powered market analysis and trading for decades, but as data grows in complexity, classical methods face limitations. Quantum computing has the potential to revolutionize financial markets by solving optimization problems faster and more efficiently than ever before.

Finding the Best Investment Strategies

Investing in financial markets requires making decisions based on many variables, such as stock prices, interest rates, economic indicators, and even social trends. One of the biggest challenges in finance is selecting the best combination of investments to maximize returns while minimizing risks—a problem known as "portfolio optimization."

Classical computers solve this problem using models that require simplifications and approximations. However, quantum computers, using their unique ability to process multiple possibilities at once, could analyze countless investment combinations in real time. This would allow financial institutions to create better investment strategies, reducing uncertainty and improving profitability.

Risk Management and Market Predictions

Financial markets are unpredictable, and managing risk is a top priority for investors. Traditional methods rely on statistical models that try to predict how markets will behave based on historical data. However, these models often struggle with sudden market shifts, such as economic crises or unexpected events.

Quantum computing could enhance risk management by analyzing a much larger set of possible market scenarios. Instead of simply looking at past data, quantum systems could simulate multiple future possibilities simultaneously. This would provide traders and financial analysts with deeper insights, helping them anticipate market fluctuations more accurately.

Faster and More Efficient Trading

High-frequency trading (HFT) firms execute thousands of trades per second, relying on advanced algorithms to identify profit opportunities. The faster a firm can process and react to information, the greater its competitive advantage.

Quantum computing has the potential to make trading algorithms even faster and more powerful. By instantly analyzing massive datasets, quantum systems could help traders detect market patterns that classical computers might miss. This speed and efficiency could redefine the competitive landscape of financial markets, making them more dynamic and efficient.

Challenges and the Future of Quantum Finance

Despite its potential, quantum computing is still in its early stages. Current quantum machines have limitations, such as high error rates and the need for extremely cold temperatures to function properly. However, researchers are making rapid progress, and major financial institutions are already exploring how quantum technology can be applied to trading, risk management, and investment strategies.

In the future, as quantum computers become more stable and powerful, they could transform financial markets in ways we can barely imagine today. From optimizing portfolios to predicting market trends with unprecedented accuracy, quantum computing holds the key to a more efficient and intelligent financial system.

The role of quantum startups and major tech companies

Quantum computing is a field filled with excitement, and both startups and major tech companies are playing key roles in its development. Each type of player brings unique strengths to the table, helping to push this revolutionary technology forward.

Startups are the pioneers of innovation in quantum computing. Unlike large corporations, they can take risks, explore new ideas, and experiment with cutting-edge techniques without being slowed down by bureaucracy. Many quantum startups focus on developing specialized hardware, software, or algorithms to solve real-world problems. Some are working on improving quantum processors, making them more stable and efficient. Others are creating software tools that will allow businesses to use quantum computers even without deep technical knowledge. These startups often rely on venture capital funding and government support to develop their technology, hoping to make breakthroughs that will change industries.

On the other hand, major tech companies like IBM, Google, Microsoft, and Amazon are heavily investing in quantum computing as well. They have the financial resources, computing power, and research teams needed to build large-scale quantum systems. Their goal is to integrate quantum computing with existing technologies, such as cloud computing and artificial intelligence. These companies are also making quantum computing more accessible by providing cloud-based platforms where businesses, researchers, and developers can experiment with quantum algorithms without needing a physical quantum computer.

The collaboration between startups and major tech companies is crucial. Large corporations often acquire promising startups or partner with them to accelerate innovation. Meanwhile, startups benefit from the financial backing, infrastructure, and expertise of these larger players.

As quantum computing continues to evolve, both startups and established tech giants will play essential roles. Startups will drive bold innovation, while major companies will ensure scalability and global impact. This dynamic ecosystem is what will ultimately bring quantum computing from research labs into practical use across industries worldwide.

10. QUANTUM COMPUTING IN EVERYDAY LIFE

Quantum computing might seem like a futuristic technology, but it has the potential to influence many aspects of daily life. While today's computers handle tasks like online shopping, banking, and entertainment, quantum computers could bring improvements that go far beyond what we currently experience. From making medical diagnoses faster to optimizing traffic systems in large cities, the power of quantum computing will help solve problems that were previously too complex.

Even if most people never directly use a quantum computer, the benefits will be felt everywhere. Companies, researchers, and governments are already working on practical applications that could change the way we live, work, and interact with technology. In this chapter, we will explore how quantum computing could transform everyday experiences, making life easier, safer, and more efficient.

Will individuals ever use quantum computers?

Most people today own a laptop, smartphone, or tablet, but will they ever have a quantum computer at home? The short answer is: probably not in the way we use regular computers today. Quantum computers work in a completely different way from traditional computers. They require highly controlled environments, such as extremely cold temperatures close to absolute zero, to function properly. This makes them impractical for home use.

However, this does not mean that individuals will not benefit from quantum computing. Just as most people do not own powerful supercomputers but still use services that rely on them, quantum computing will likely be accessed through the internet. Companies and researchers are already working on cloud-based quantum computing, where users can run quantum-powered applications without needing to own a quantum computer themselves.

In the future, quantum technology could enhance many aspects of everyday digital life. It could improve online security, optimize search engines, and make artificial intelligence smarter and more efficient. While people may not directly use quantum computers at home, they will experience their impact in ways they might not even realize—through faster problem-solving, better predictions, and more advanced technologies that make life easier.

Potential improvements in consumer technology

Quantum computing has the potential to transform the technology people use every day. Even though most individuals will never own a quantum computer, they will still benefit from its capabilities. One of the most exciting possibilities is how quantum computing could improve devices such as smartphones, computers, and even smart home systems.

For example, artificial intelligence (AI) is already a major part of modern consumer technology. Voice assistants, recommendation systems, and smart devices rely on AI to understand and predict user needs. Quantum computing could make AI much more powerful by processing vast amounts of data faster and finding better solutions. This could mean voice assistants that understand natural speech even better, personalized recommendations that are far more accurate, and smart home systems that can optimize energy use based on real-time conditions.

Another area that could see major improvements is cybersecurity. As online threats become more sophisticated, traditional encryption methods will eventually become less secure. Quantum computers will be able to create new encryption techniques that are nearly impossible to break, protecting personal information, online transactions, and digital communications. In a world where people increasingly rely on digital payments and cloud storage, having stronger security will be crucial.

Quantum technology could also improve the speed and efficiency of search engines, making it easier to find relevant information instantly. Navigation systems could become more accurate, helping people reach their destinations faster with better traffic predictions. Even battery life in electronic devices could benefit, as quantum-powered simulations might help design more efficient batteries for smartphones, laptops, and electric vehicles.

While quantum computers themselves may remain in research labs and data centers, the improvements they bring to consumer technology will shape everyday experiences in ways most people will take for granted. Faster, smarter, and more secure devices will become a reality, all thanks to the power of quantum computing.

How it could change daily decision-making

Every day, people make countless decisions—what route to take to work, which product to buy, or even what to eat for dinner. While these choices may seem simple, they often involve many factors: time, cost, availability, and personal preferences. Quantum computing has the potential to make daily decision-making easier and more efficient by providing faster, smarter, and more personalized recommendations.

One major area where quantum computing could help is **navigation and travel planning**. Today, apps like Google Maps and Waze use algorithms to suggest the best route based on traffic conditions. However, these systems still rely on classical computing, which has limitations when dealing with real-time changes, such as sudden road closures or unpredictable weather. Quantum computing could analyze vast amounts of data instantly, providing more accurate and dynamic recommendations to help people get to their destinations faster and with fewer delays.

Shopping decisions could also improve. Whether buying groceries, electronics, or booking a vacation, people often compare prices, check reviews, and consider multiple options. Quantum computing could power more advanced recommendation systems that take into account not just price and quality but also personal preferences, real-time demand, and future trends. This could help consumers find the best deals and make informed choices without spending hours researching.

Health and wellness is another area where quantum computing could enhance decision-making. Wearable health devices and fitness apps already track heart rates, sleep patterns, and activity levels. In the future, quantum-powered AI could analyze this data in real time, offering personalized health recommendations. Imagine an app that instantly suggests the best diet or workout based on a person's unique metabolism, stress levels, and daily schedule. This could lead to smarter lifestyle choices that improve long-term well-being.

Even something as simple as **planning a daily schedule** could become more efficient. Today, calendar apps help people organize their time, but they often require manual input. With quantum computing, personal assistants could analyze an individual's habits, work commitments, and even mood patterns to create the most optimized schedule. This could lead to less stress, better productivity, and more free time for personal activities.

While quantum computing may seem like a technology of the future, its impact on daily decision-making could be profound. From helping people navigate their cities to making smarter purchases and improving their health, quantum-driven solutions could bring convenience and efficiency to everyday life in ways that are only beginning to be imagined.

11. QUANTUM COMPUTING AND EDUCATION

Education has always evolved with technology, from the printing press to the internet. Now, quantum computing promises to bring another transformation. While it may seem like a complex scientific field, its impact on education could be significant. Schools and universities will need to prepare students for a future where quantum skills are valuable, just as they did with computers and programming in the past.

Beyond teaching quantum computing itself, this technology could also change how students learn. Faster data analysis, personalized learning experiences, and advanced simulations could make education more interactive and efficient. In this chapter, we will explore how quantum computing might reshape classrooms, research, and the way knowledge is shared across the world.

How quantum literacy will become a necessity

In the past, understanding computers was optional. Only scientists and engineers needed to know how they worked. But as computers became a part of daily life, digital literacy became essential. The same shift is beginning with quantum computing. While not everyone will need to be a quantum physicist, having basic knowledge of how quantum computers function and what they can do will become increasingly important.

Quantum computing has the potential to influence many areas of life, from finance to medicine. Imagine a doctor using quantum-powered simulations to find the best treatment for a disease or a business leader making decisions based on quantum-enhanced data analysis. Without a basic understanding of how quantum computing works, people may struggle to fully grasp the benefits, risks, and opportunities it presents.

Education systems will need to adapt. Just as schools introduced coding into their curricula, they may soon teach fundamental quantum concepts. Students might learn about qubits, superposition, and quantum algorithms in the same way they currently learn about classical computing and programming. Universities will expand their quantum computing programs, not just for scientists, but for students in business, healthcare, and other fields that will be affected by this technology.

Even outside of formal education, quantum literacy will play a role in everyday decision-making. Businesses will have to assess whether investing in quantum technology makes sense. Consumers will need to understand the impact of quantum computing on data security and privacy. Governments and policymakers will be responsible for regulating quantum advancements in a way that benefits society. Without basic quantum literacy, people could find themselves unable to make informed choices in a world where quantum computing plays a growing role.

The good news is that learning about quantum computing does not require deep expertise in physics or mathematics. Simple explanations, interactive tools, and educational programs will make it accessible to a broad audience. Just as the internet made digital learning possible for millions, quantum computing will inspire new ways of teaching and understanding complex ideas. In the future, knowing the basics of quantum computing may be as natural as understanding how the internet works today.

New educational programs and career opportunities

Quantum computing is still a new field, but it is growing fast. As companies and governments invest in quantum technology, the need for skilled professionals is increasing. This demand is shaping education, leading to the creation of new programs and career opportunities.

Many universities around the world are introducing quantum computing courses. Some offer specialized degrees, while others include quantum topics in existing computer science or physics programs. These courses teach students the basics of quantum mechanics, programming for quantum computers, and how quantum algorithms differ from traditional computing methods. In the future, quantum computing may become a standard part of science and engineering education, just like classical computing is today.

Beyond universities, online learning platforms and tech companies are offering training programs. Some are designed for professionals who want to switch careers or expand their knowledge. Others are for students and beginners who want to understand how quantum computing works. These programs use interactive tools, simulations, and cloud-based quantum processors to help learners gain hands-on experience.

Career opportunities in quantum computing are also expanding. While research and development still require highly specialized skills, new job roles are emerging. Businesses need experts who can apply quantum technology to real-world problems. Financial institutions, for example, are looking for quantum analysts to improve market predictions. Pharmaceutical companies are hiring quantum researchers to develop new drugs. Governments and cybersecurity firms need quantum specialists to prepare for the impact of quantum computing on encryption and data security.

For those interested in technology but not in deep physics, there are also opportunities. Quantum software developers, system architects, and data scientists will play key roles in making quantum computing practical for businesses. Even non-technical fields will be affected— lawyers, policymakers, and business leaders will need to understand quantum computing to make informed decisions.

The rise of quantum computing education means that people of different backgrounds will have the chance to enter this exciting field. Whether through traditional degrees, online courses, or specialized training, learning about quantum computing will open doors to new career paths. As the technology evolves, the demand for quantum-literate professionals will only grow, making it an important area of study for the future.

The importance of interdisciplinary learning

Quantum computing is not just about physics or mathematics. It brings together ideas from different fields, creating a new way of thinking about technology and problem-solving. To fully understand and use quantum computing, students and professionals must learn from multiple disciplines. This is why interdisciplinary learning is so important in this field.

At its core, quantum computing is based on quantum mechanics, a branch of physics that describes how tiny particles behave. However, understanding quantum mechanics alone is not enough. To build and use quantum computers, knowledge of computer science is essential. Programming a quantum computer requires new types of algorithms that work in ways completely different from traditional computers. This is why experts in artificial intelligence and software development are also needed in quantum research.

Mathematics plays a key role as well. Quantum computing relies on complex mathematical concepts, such as linear algebra and probability theory, to describe how quantum bits (qubits) behave. Without a strong mathematical foundation, it would be difficult to design quantum algorithms or predict how a quantum system will respond in different situations.

Beyond science and technology, other disciplines also contribute to quantum computing. In business and finance, quantum computing is expected to transform industries by solving optimization problems faster than classical computers. This means that economists, financial analysts, and business leaders will need a basic understanding of quantum technology to stay competitive.

Cybersecurity is another important area. As quantum computers become more powerful, they will be able to break many of the encryption methods used today. Governments, law enforcement agencies, and cybersecurity experts must work together to develop new ways to protect sensitive information.

Even philosophy and ethics have a role in quantum computing. The potential power of this technology raises important ethical questions about privacy, security, and fairness. Discussions about how quantum computing should be used will require input from ethicists, policymakers, and legal experts.

Interdisciplinary learning is not just about combining knowledge from different fields—it is about creating a mindset that allows people to approach complex problems from multiple angles. As quantum computing continues to evolve, those who can bridge the gap between different disciplines will have the most impact. This is why future education in quantum computing must encourage collaboration across fields, ensuring that experts from different backgrounds can work together to unlock the full potential of this revolutionary technology.

12. QUANTUM COMPUTING AND THE LABOR MARKET

Quantum computing is not just a breakthrough in technology—it's also creating new job opportunities and reshaping industries. As this technology develops, the demand for skilled professionals in quantum computing is growing rapidly. But it's not just for physicists and computer scientists; people from many fields will need to adapt and learn how to work alongside quantum systems. This chapter will explore how quantum computing is influencing the labor market, what kinds of jobs are emerging, and how workers can prepare for the changes ahead. Whether you're a student or a professional, understanding this shift is key to staying relevant in the workforce of the future.

Job displacement vs. job creation

As quantum computing continues to develop, one of the key questions is how it will impact jobs. Will it lead to job displacement, where certain roles become obsolete? Or will it create new opportunities and transform existing industries in ways that we can't yet fully understand?

In many ways, quantum computing could lead to job displacement in some areas, especially in fields that rely heavily on traditional computing methods. For example, certain tasks that today require long hours of data analysis or complex calculations could be handled much faster by quantum computers. This could mean a reduced need for workers in these specific areas. Jobs that focus on routine and repetitive tasks, which quantum computers can perform more efficiently, may be at risk.

However, the displacement of jobs doesn't necessarily mean a net loss for workers. While quantum computing could change the nature of certain roles, it will also create entirely new opportunities. The rise of quantum technology will require a new generation of quantum engineers, researchers, and specialists to build, maintain, and optimize quantum systems. Additionally, industries like pharmaceuticals, materials science, and cryptography will need experts who can apply quantum computing to real-world challenges.

Quantum computing also offers the potential to revolutionize existing fields. For example, in finance, quantum algorithms could be used to analyze vast amounts of data and optimize investment strategies. This will require not only computer scientists but also professionals who understand finance and can apply quantum tools to improve decision-making.

Moreover, as quantum computing becomes more integrated into various sectors, there will be an increasing need for people who can bridge the gap between quantum technology and industries like healthcare, logistics, and education. This means that professionals with an understanding of both quantum computing and other fields will be in high demand.

In conclusion, while quantum computing may lead to job displacement in some areas, it is also poised to create new opportunities in many others. Workers who are adaptable and willing to learn will find themselves at the forefront of a growing and exciting field.

The rise of new professions in the quantum era

As quantum computing grows, it is not only transforming industries but also creating a new landscape of careers that didn't exist before. The demand for new skill sets is driving the rise of professions that combine quantum physics with technology, business, and even the arts. These new professions are shaping the future of the workforce, with exciting opportunities for those willing to learn and adapt.

One of the most obvious new roles is the **quantum software developer**. As quantum computers become more powerful, there will be a need for people who can write software specifically designed to run on these machines. Quantum computers work in ways that traditional computers do not, which means regular coding skills are not enough. Developers will need to understand quantum algorithms and how to translate problems into a quantum language. This field is still in its early stages, but as quantum computers evolve, so too will the demand for developers with specialized knowledge.

Alongside quantum software developers, we are seeing the growth of **quantum hardware engineers**. These professionals are responsible for designing, building, and maintaining quantum computing systems. The hardware of quantum computers is fundamentally different from traditional computers, relying on principles of quantum mechanics like superposition and entanglement. Engineers in this field will need a deep understanding of both the science of quantum mechanics and the practicalities of building machines that can manipulate quantum bits, or qubits, which are the fundamental units of information in quantum computers.

Quantum data scientists are another new profession arising from the quantum era. Data science is already a booming field, but quantum computing will take it to the next level. Quantum computers can process enormous amounts of data far faster than classical computers, enabling scientists to solve complex problems in fields like medicine, climate science, and financial modeling. Quantum data scientists will need to know how to work with both quantum computing systems and massive datasets, helping organizations unlock insights and solve problems that were previously out of reach.

Another emerging profession is the **quantum cybersecurity expert**. With quantum computers on the horizon, traditional encryption methods used to protect our sensitive information, such as online banking or personal data, may become vulnerable. Quantum computers could break many of the current encryption techniques. As a result, there will be an increasing demand for experts in quantum cryptography, who can develop new methods of protecting data against quantum attacks. These professionals will play a crucial role in ensuring the safety and privacy of digital communications in the quantum age.

Moreover, as quantum computing grows in importance, the demand for **quantum consultants** will rise. These professionals will help businesses and governments understand the potential of quantum computing for their specific industries. They will work on solving problems such as how quantum computing can improve supply chains, optimize energy usage, or accelerate research and development. Quantum consultants will bridge the gap between complex quantum technologies and practical business applications, making them key players in helping industries adapt to the quantum revolution.

In addition to technical roles, new jobs will emerge in the education and training sectors. **Quantum educators** will be needed to teach the next generation of quantum professionals, ranging from university professors to corporate trainers. With quantum computing still in its early stages, many universities and online platforms are beginning to offer specialized courses to equip students with the necessary skills to enter this growing field. Educators will also help non-technical people understand how quantum technology might impact their industries or daily lives.

Finally, the field of quantum ethics will give rise to **quantum ethicists**—professionals who will focus on the social, legal, and ethical implications of quantum technologies. As quantum computers will have the potential to change everything from privacy laws to social inequality, ethicists will play an essential role in guiding how quantum technology is developed and used in a responsible and ethical way.

In summary, the rise of quantum computing is not just about new technology, but also about the creation of exciting, dynamic careers. As quantum technology continues to evolve, the professions in the quantum era will transform the workforce. Those who understand the unique demands of quantum computing, whether it's building machines, analyzing data, or protecting information, will find themselves at the center of a rapidly growing and highly impactful field.

How businesses will adapt to a quantum-driven economy

As quantum computing begins to make its mark on the world, businesses must adapt to this rapidly changing landscape to stay competitive. While quantum computing may still seem distant for many, its impact is likely to be felt much sooner than anticipated. To understand how businesses will adapt, it's important to recognize that quantum computing will unlock capabilities that traditional computers cannot match. This will transform industries ranging from healthcare and finance to logistics and energy.

For businesses, the first step in adapting to a quantum-driven economy will be to **understand the potential applications** of quantum technology. Quantum computers have the ability to process vast amounts of data simultaneously, making them ideal for solving complex problems that traditional computers struggle with. For example, in **finance**, quantum computing could improve risk management models, optimize investment strategies, and enable faster processing of financial transactions. Companies in this sector will need to invest in **quantum research** and build partnerships with quantum technology providers to harness these capabilities.

Another area where businesses will see change is in **optimization**. Quantum computers are particularly powerful when it comes to finding the most efficient solutions to problems, such as optimizing supply chains, scheduling, or energy usage. Companies in manufacturing, logistics, and energy management can leverage quantum computing to streamline their operations, reduce costs, and improve overall performance. For instance, in **transportation**, quantum algorithms could optimize delivery routes in real-time, minimizing fuel consumption and delivery times. Businesses in these sectors will need to adopt new strategies and invest in **quantum-ready infrastructure** to integrate quantum computing into their operations.

As quantum computing advances, businesses will also need to **develop new business models**. Quantum computing's potential will lead to the creation of entirely new products and services. Companies that are early adopters of quantum technologies will have the chance to develop **innovative offerings** that no one else can provide. For example, in **drug discovery**, quantum computers could model complex molecules and reactions at an atomic level, potentially accelerating the development of new medications. Pharmaceutical companies, healthcare providers, and biotech firms must stay ahead of the curve by investing in quantum technologies and creating teams dedicated to exploring the quantum potential in their industries.

Moreover, the **workforce** will have to evolve. Businesses will need to develop strategies for **quantum talent acquisition** and ensure that their teams are equipped with the knowledge to navigate the new quantum landscape. Companies will likely need to hire **quantum specialists**, such as quantum software developers and hardware engineers, to support the integration of quantum computing into their operations. At the same time, businesses must provide **training programs** to help existing employees develop new skills and understand how quantum technology will affect their roles. Adapting to a quantum-driven economy means that employees across various sectors must become **quantum-literate** to some extent, even if they are not directly working with quantum computers.

As quantum technology becomes more accessible, businesses will also need to adopt **cloud-based quantum services**. Since building and maintaining quantum hardware is expensive and complex, many companies will opt to use quantum computing as a service through the cloud. Cloud providers will offer access to quantum processors, enabling businesses of all sizes to run quantum algorithms without having to invest in their own hardware. This opens up opportunities for **smaller businesses** to take advantage of quantum computing without having to make significant capital investments upfront.

In addition, **collaboration** will play a key role in how businesses adapt to quantum computing. The complexities of quantum technology mean that no single company can master it on its own. Therefore, businesses will likely form **strategic alliances** with academic institutions, tech giants, and startups specializing in quantum computing. These collaborations will allow businesses to share knowledge, resources, and expertise, accelerating the development of quantum solutions and ensuring that they stay ahead in the quantum race.

Finally, businesses will need to **embrace change and flexibility**. The quantum revolution will not happen overnight, but it will unfold over the next few decades, and companies must be ready to adjust their strategies as quantum computing evolves. This means fostering a culture of innovation and encouraging experimentation. As quantum technology becomes integrated into various industries, businesses that remain flexible and adaptable will be the ones to thrive in the quantum-driven economy.

In conclusion, businesses will adapt to a quantum-driven economy by understanding the potential applications of quantum computing, adopting new business models, developing quantum talent, leveraging cloud-based quantum services, collaborating with other organizations, and fostering a culture of flexibility and innovation. Companies that take the lead in exploring quantum technologies will be well-positioned to capitalize on the groundbreaking opportunities that this new era of computing offers.

13. QUANTUM COMPUTING AND INDIVIDUAL FREEDOM

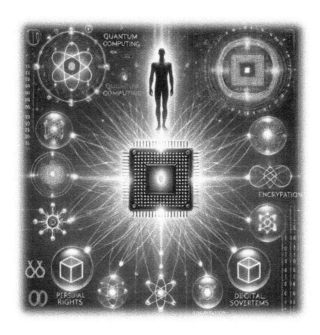

Technology has always influenced personal freedom, shaping the way we communicate, work, and protect our privacy. Quantum computing, with its ability to process information at an unprecedented scale, raises new questions about how much control individuals will have over their data, security, and even their choices in a world driven by powerful algorithms. Will quantum computing strengthen individual freedom by offering better encryption and security? Or will it create new risks by making personal data more vulnerable? As we enter the quantum age, it is crucial to explore how this technology will impact our rights, privacy, and independence.

Risks of mass surveillance and data control

The development of quantum computing brings both exciting possibilities and serious concerns. Among the most pressing issues is the risk of mass surveillance and data control. In a world where governments, corporations, and other entities already collect vast amounts of personal information, quantum technology could take this to an entirely new level.

One of the reasons quantum computing raises concerns is its ability to break current encryption methods. Today, much of our private communication—emails, financial transactions, and even medical records—is protected by encryption. However, quantum computers could decode this encryption in a matter of seconds, making it possible for those with access to quantum technology to see information that was once considered secure. This could lead to a future where private data is no longer truly private.

Beyond encryption, quantum computing could also enhance artificial intelligence and data analysis in ways that increase surveillance. Governments and companies already use AI to monitor internet activity, predict consumer behavior, and even track individuals through facial recognition. If combined with quantum-powered processing, these technologies could become far more invasive. A government with access to such capabilities could monitor an entire population in real time, making it almost impossible for citizens to communicate freely without the risk of being watched.

Another concern is the concentration of power. Quantum computing is expensive and requires specialized knowledge. Unlike personal computers or smartphones, which are accessible to most people, quantum technology is currently limited to large organizations, wealthy corporations, and state agencies. This creates an imbalance where only a few powerful entities control the most advanced computing capabilities, making them capable of exerting influence over societies in ways never seen before.

The ability to process massive amounts of data at unprecedented speeds could also be used to manipulate public opinion. Quantum-enhanced AI could analyze social media, news trends, and personal messages to shape political discourse, influence elections, or suppress dissent. If used irresponsibly, such technology could restrict freedom of expression and limit people's ability to form independent opinions.

To protect individual freedom in the quantum age, new strategies will be needed. Researchers are already developing quantum-resistant encryption methods, which aim to safeguard data even in a world with powerful quantum computers. At the same time, legal and ethical discussions are necessary to ensure that quantum technology does not become a tool of mass surveillance and control.

As with any powerful technology, quantum computing has the potential to improve lives or threaten fundamental rights. The choices made today in terms of regulation, privacy protection, and ethical responsibility will determine whether this new era enhances individual freedom or limits it. The challenge will be to embrace the benefits of quantum computing while ensuring that personal data, privacy, and freedom remain protected.

The ethical debate on who controls quantum computing

Quantum computing is not just a technological revolution; it is also a matter of power, ethics, and control. Because this technology has the potential to change the world, the question arises: Who should control it? Should it be in the hands of private companies, governments, or international organizations? The answer to this question will shape the future of individual freedom, economic balance, and global security.

At the moment, only a few entities have access to quantum technology. Large tech companies, such as Google, IBM, and Microsoft, are leading research, while governments—especially those of the United States, China, and the European Union—are investing heavily in quantum development. The cost of building and maintaining quantum computers is extremely high, which means that only the wealthiest players can afford to develop them. This creates a gap between those who control quantum computing and the rest of society.

If private companies dominate quantum computing, ethical concerns emerge. These companies operate with profit in mind, and there is no guarantee that they will use quantum technology for the benefit of everyone. A corporation could use quantum computing to strengthen its competitive advantage, manipulate markets, or collect vast amounts of personal data. Without strong regulations, individuals might lose control over their digital privacy and economic opportunities.

On the other hand, if governments control quantum computing, different risks arise. Some governments could use quantum technology for mass surveillance, espionage, or military advantage. The ability to break encryption could allow authorities to monitor private communications, exposing individuals to unprecedented levels of state control. In authoritarian regimes, this could limit personal freedom, making it difficult for people to express dissent or organize opposition. Even in democratic countries, there is a risk that quantum technology could be used in ways that violate privacy and civil liberties.

An alternative approach would be to place quantum computing under international cooperation. Some experts argue that, like nuclear technology, quantum computing should be regulated by global agreements. If multiple countries and organizations work together, it could reduce the risk of any one entity having too much power. However, history has shown that global agreements are difficult to enforce, and powerful nations may not be willing to share control.

The ethical debate also extends to access. Should quantum computing be open to everyone, or should it be restricted? Some believe that making quantum technology publicly available could drive innovation and economic progress. Others argue that unrestricted access could lead to dangerous consequences, such as cybercriminals using quantum computers to break security systems.

Ultimately, the debate over who controls quantum computing is about trust, responsibility, and fairness. The challenge is to find a balance between innovation and protection, between progress and security. Society must decide whether quantum computing will be a tool for collective advancement or a weapon for those in power. The choices made today will determine whether quantum computing becomes a force for freedom or a tool of control.

Balancing innovation with personal privacy

Quantum computing promises to transform the world in ways we are only beginning to understand. It has the potential to revolutionize medicine, finance, and artificial intelligence, solving problems that are currently impossible for traditional computers. However, as with any powerful technology, there is a challenge: how can we encourage innovation while also protecting personal privacy?

One of the biggest concerns is data security. Quantum computers will eventually be able to break many of the encryption systems used today to protect personal information. This means that emails, banking details, and even government secrets could become vulnerable. Without new security measures, quantum computing could expose people to identity theft, financial fraud, and mass surveillance.

At the same time, quantum computing could also create new ways to protect privacy. Researchers are developing quantum encryption methods that would be nearly impossible to hack. This means that if used correctly, quantum technology could actually strengthen privacy rather than weaken it. The key question is: who will control these technologies? If they are used responsibly, they could protect individuals. But if they fall into the wrong hands, they could be used for large-scale surveillance.

Governments and companies will play a major role in defining the balance between progress and privacy. Businesses want access to the most advanced computing power to improve their services, make better predictions, and increase profits. Governments, especially intelligence and law enforcement agencies, want to use quantum computing to track criminal activities and prevent cyber threats. These interests often conflict with personal freedom.

Regulation will be crucial in ensuring that quantum innovation does not come at the expense of individual rights. Laws must be updated to define what can and cannot be done with quantum computing, just as past regulations were created for the internet and artificial intelligence. Without proper legal frameworks, there is a risk that companies and governments will push the boundaries of what is ethical, putting personal freedoms at risk.

Another important factor is public awareness. People must understand what quantum computing is and how it could impact their privacy. When individuals are informed, they can demand better protections, support ethical policies, and make choices that safeguard their data. For example, they can choose services that prioritize quantum-safe encryption or advocate for laws that protect digital rights.

Finding a balance between innovation and privacy is not easy, but it is necessary. The challenge is to encourage the development of quantum technology in a way that benefits society while preventing it from being misused. The decisions made today will shape the future of digital freedom, determining whether quantum computing becomes a force for empowerment or a tool of control.

14. QUANTUM COMPUTING AND GEOPOLITICS

Quantum computing is not just a scientific breakthrough; it is also a powerful tool that could shift the balance of global power. Countries around the world are racing to develop this technology, knowing that whoever leads in quantum computing will gain a major strategic advantage. From national security to economic dominance, the impact of quantum computing will go far beyond laboratories and universities.

This new technological race is shaping international relations, creating new alliances and rivalries. Governments are investing billions to ensure they do not fall behind, while some nations are restricting access to quantum research to protect their own interests. Just as nuclear technology changed global politics in the 20th century, quantum computing is set to redefine power dynamics in the 21st. The question is: who will control this technology, and how will it shape the future of international affairs?

The race for quantum supremacy

The competition to develop the most powerful quantum computers is not just a technological challenge—it is a global race that could reshape the balance of power. Governments and major corporations are investing billions of dollars into quantum research, hoping to be the first to achieve what is called *quantum supremacy*. This term refers to the moment when a quantum computer can solve a problem that even the best classical computers cannot handle within a reasonable time.

The stakes are enormous. The country or organization that reaches quantum supremacy first will gain significant advantages in many fields, including cybersecurity, artificial intelligence, and financial modeling. Quantum computers could break current encryption methods, making classified information vulnerable. They could also revolutionize materials science, leading to breakthroughs in energy, medicine, and defense technologies.

The United States, China, the European Union, and other global powers are deeply engaged in this race. The U.S. government has allocated significant funding for quantum research, recognizing its importance for national security. China, on the other hand, has made quantum computing a key part of its technological strategy, investing in quantum networks and research centers. Europe is also pushing forward with large-scale projects, aiming to remain competitive in the field.

This race is not just about scientific progress; it is also about influence and control. A country with advanced quantum technology could dominate industries, secure its communications, and even disrupt the digital infrastructure of other nations. Because of this, many governments are tightening restrictions on quantum research, limiting the sharing of knowledge and technology to prevent rivals from gaining an advantage.

However, some experts believe that quantum supremacy will not belong to a single country or company. Collaboration across borders could accelerate discoveries, leading to shared benefits rather than a winner-takes-all scenario. But the political reality is different—nations are cautious, and many see quantum computing as a strategic asset that must be protected.

As the race for quantum supremacy continues, the world is entering a new era where technology and geopolitics are deeply intertwined. The question remains: will quantum computing be a tool for global cooperation, or will it deepen divisions between nations?

The role of governments and defense sectors

Quantum computing is not just an academic pursuit or a commercial opportunity—it is also a matter of national security. Governments around the world are investing heavily in quantum research, recognizing that this technology could give them a significant advantage in areas such as cybersecurity, intelligence, and military strategy.

One of the most urgent concerns is encryption. Today's internet security relies on complex mathematical problems that classical computers cannot solve quickly. Quantum computers, however, have the potential to break these encryption methods, making sensitive government and military communications vulnerable. To counter this threat, defense agencies are working on **quantum-resistant encryption**, which could protect data even in a world where quantum computers are widely available.

Beyond cybersecurity, quantum computing could enhance intelligence gathering. Governments and intelligence agencies process vast amounts of data every day. Quantum technology could help analyze patterns, decrypt messages, and even predict threats more effectively than ever before. A nation with superior quantum capabilities might be able to monitor global communications with unprecedented speed and accuracy.

Military applications are another major focus. Quantum computers could optimize complex logistical operations, improve real-time battlefield decisions, and enhance the development of advanced weapons systems. Some countries are even exploring the use of **quantum sensors**, which could detect submarines, stealth aircraft, or hidden military movements more accurately than traditional radar systems.

Because of these possibilities, leading world powers—including the United States, China, the European Union, and Russia—are treating quantum computing as a **strategic priority**. Billions of dollars are being allocated to research programs, and partnerships between governments, universities, and private companies are forming to accelerate progress. However, not all research is shared. Many breakthroughs in quantum computing are classified, and governments are imposing strict regulations on who can access certain technologies.

This secrecy raises important geopolitical questions. If only a few nations control quantum computing, could they use it to dominate weaker economies or interfere in global affairs? Will quantum technology create new alliances, or will it deepen the divide between technological superpowers and less-developed nations?

At the same time, some believe that quantum computing should be a global effort. International collaborations, such as agreements between research institutions and cross-border partnerships, could ensure that quantum progress benefits humanity as a whole rather than just a few powerful nations. However, history has shown that when technology has military or strategic value, governments tend to keep it under tight control.

As quantum computing advances, the role of governments and defense sectors will only grow. The challenge will be to harness this powerful technology while preventing it from becoming a tool for domination and conflict. Will quantum computing bring nations together, or will it become the next battlefield in global competition? The answer to this question may define the future of international relations.

How quantum computing could shift global power dynamics

Throughout history, technological breakthroughs have reshaped global power structures. The steam engine fueled the Industrial Revolution, nuclear weapons changed the balance of military strength, and the internet transformed economies and communication. Quantum computing could be the next game-changing technology, potentially redistributing power among nations in ways we are only beginning to understand.

One of the most immediate impacts could be in the field of **cybersecurity**. Today, many countries rely on encryption to protect classified information, financial transactions, and critical infrastructure. Quantum computers, however, could break most of these encryption methods in a matter of minutes, rendering current security systems obsolete. Nations that achieve quantum supremacy first may gain an enormous advantage, being able to decode sensitive communications while keeping their own data safe through quantum-resistant encryption. This shift alone could place some countries at the top of the geopolitical hierarchy while leaving others vulnerable.

Beyond cybersecurity, **economic power could be redistributed**. Quantum computers will allow businesses to solve complex problems faster than ever before, revolutionizing industries such as pharmaceuticals, materials science, and finance. Nations that develop and control quantum technology will have a head start in medical research, enabling them to create life-saving drugs more efficiently. They will also be able to optimize supply chains, enhance energy efficiency, and predict market movements with incredible precision. Countries that lag behind in this quantum race may struggle to keep up economically, deepening the divide between technological superpowers and developing nations.

Another key area of change is **military strategy**. Warfare has always been influenced by technology, from gunpowder to artificial intelligence. Quantum computing could introduce a new level of strategic planning, allowing militaries to simulate and predict battle scenarios with unprecedented accuracy. Quantum-powered simulations could enhance defense systems, improve logistics, and even make autonomous weapons more intelligent. The nations that master these applications will hold an undeniable strategic edge.

Geopolitical alliances may also shift as countries seek to **cooperate or compete** in quantum research. Some nations will form partnerships to share knowledge and accelerate progress, while others will adopt a more secretive approach to maintain their competitive advantage. We are already seeing early signs of this dynamic, with the United States, China, and the European Union investing billions into quantum research. Some governments are restricting access to quantum technologies, treating them as classified resources rather than shared scientific discoveries.

However, quantum computing is not just a tool for dominance—it could also serve as a **bridge for diplomacy**. Just as space exploration has led to international cooperation, quantum research could inspire new global partnerships. Some scientists argue that an open and collaborative approach would be the best way to ensure that quantum computing benefits humanity as a whole rather than just a few elite nations.

Ultimately, quantum computing has the potential to **redraw the world map of power**. It could lead to new economic leaders, disrupt global security, and create both conflicts and alliances. Whether it will be used for progress or control depends on the choices made today. The race for quantum dominance is not just about technology—it is about the future balance of power on a global scale.

15. ETHICAL AND PHILOSOPHICAL QUESTIONS

Quantum computing is not just about speed and power; it also raises deep ethical and philosophical questions. Who should control this technology? How can we ensure it is used for good rather than harm? Will it increase fairness in society, or will it deepen inequalities? These are not just technical issues but moral dilemmas that will shape the future of humanity. As we explore the potential of quantum computing, we must also consider its impact on privacy, security, decision-making, and even our understanding of reality itself.

Who should have access to quantum technology?

Quantum computing is a powerful tool that has the potential to reshape industries, economies, and even global politics. But one of the most important questions we must ask is: who should have access to this technology? Should it be reserved for governments and large corporations, or should it be available to universities, startups, and even individual researchers?

If only a few powerful entities control quantum computing, they could use it for their own advantage, widening the gap between the rich and the poor, the strong and the weak. This could lead to economic monopolies, stronger surveillance systems, and even military applications that could make global conflicts more unpredictable.

On the other hand, if quantum technology is made widely available, there is a risk that it could be misused. Criminal organizations could exploit it for cyberattacks, breaking encryption that protects financial transactions and personal data. Some fear that if quantum computing becomes too accessible, it could destabilize the security systems that keep the digital world running.

A balanced approach might be the best solution. Governments and regulatory bodies could ensure that quantum computing is used responsibly, while universities and research institutions could continue to develop its potential for solving important scientific problems.

Ethical guidelines will be necessary to prevent misuse while encouraging innovation.

Ultimately, quantum computing should be a tool for progress, not a weapon of control or exclusion. The challenge lies in creating a system where access to this technology benefits humanity as a whole, rather than serving only the interests of a privileged few.

The risk of unintended consequences

Quantum computing promises to solve some of humanity's biggest challenges, from drug discovery to climate modeling. However, like any powerful technology, it also carries risks—especially those we may not yet fully understand. History has shown that major technological advances often come with unintended consequences. The internet, for example, brought incredible connectivity but also new forms of crime, misinformation, and privacy concerns. Artificial intelligence is revolutionizing industries but also raises questions about bias, job displacement, and ethical decision-making. Quantum computing could follow a similar path, delivering groundbreaking benefits while creating unforeseen challenges.

One major risk is the impact on cybersecurity. Quantum computers will be able to break today's encryption methods, which currently protect everything from personal emails to bank transactions. While researchers are developing new quantum-resistant encryption, there is no guarantee that governments, corporations, or criminals won't exploit the weaknesses before better security measures are in place.

Another possible consequence is economic disruption. Quantum computing could dramatically accelerate financial modeling, supply chain management, and optimization processes. While this might sound beneficial, it could also lead to sudden shifts in global markets, favoring those who have access to quantum resources while leaving others struggling to adapt. Entire industries could be restructured overnight, leading to job losses and economic imbalances.

There are also ethical concerns regarding artificial intelligence. If AI is enhanced by quantum computing, it could make decisions far more complex than humans can understand. This could lead to systems that make choices without transparency or accountability. Governments and corporations could use such technology for surveillance, social control, or even autonomous decision-making in warfare, raising deep moral questions.

Perhaps the most unpredictable risks come from scientific discoveries that quantum computing may unlock. Some experts believe it could lead to breakthroughs in materials science, energy, or even biological research. But what if these discoveries introduce dangers—such as the ability to manipulate genes in ways we cannot yet control, or the creation of materials that have unknown, possibly harmful effects on the environment?

The challenge with unintended consequences is that they often become clear only after the technology is widely used. That is why it is crucial to think ahead, to create ethical guidelines, regulations, and safety measures before quantum computing becomes mainstream. We must ensure that the benefits outweigh the risks, and that this technology serves humanity rather than threatening it.

How it can challenge our understanding of reality

Quantum computing is not just a technological revolution; it is also a window into the strange and mysterious nature of reality. Unlike classical computers, which process information in a predictable and logical way, quantum computers operate based on the principles of quantum mechanics—a branch of physics that defies our everyday intuition. This raises profound questions about the nature of existence, the limits of human knowledge, and even the structure of reality itself.

One of the most challenging concepts in quantum mechanics is **superposition**. In simple terms, a quantum bit (or qubit) can exist in multiple states at once, rather than just being a 0 or a 1 like a traditional bit. This means that, at a fundamental level, reality is not as fixed as we once thought. Instead of clear, definite states, things can exist in a kind of "blurred" condition until they are measured. Does this mean reality itself is uncertain until we observe it? If so, what does that say about the nature of the universe and our role as observers?

Another mind-bending principle is **entanglement**. When two quantum particles become entangled, their states become linked, no matter how far apart they are. A change in one particle instantly affects the other, even if they are light-years apart. This challenges our classical understanding of space and time. How can information travel instantaneously across vast distances? Some scientists believe this hints at a deeper level of reality that we do not yet understand—perhaps even a hidden structure of the universe that connects everything in ways beyond our current scientific models.

Quantum computing forces us to reconsider the very concept of **determinism**. In the classical world, everything follows strict cause-and-effect rules. If we know all the initial conditions, we can predict future events with certainty. But in the quantum world, things are governed by probabilities rather than certainties. Even with complete knowledge of a system, we can only predict the likelihood of different outcomes, not exact results. This has major implications for how we think about free will, randomness, and the nature of time itself.

There are also philosophical questions about **parallel realities**. Some interpretations of quantum mechanics suggest that every time a quantum system makes a choice, the universe splits into multiple versions, each representing a different outcome. If this is true, quantum computing might be operating across multiple realities at once. Could this mean that countless versions of us exist in parallel worlds? And if so, what does that mean for our sense of identity and existence?

Quantum computing is not just a faster way to process information. It is a tool that forces us to rethink everything we know about reality. As this technology advances, it may provide new insights into the universe, consciousness, and even the fundamental nature of existence. But for now, it leaves us with more questions than answers—questions that challenge the very foundation of human understanding.

16. CONCLUSION: THE FUTURE OF COMPUTING

The journey of computing has been one of constant evolution, from simple mechanical machines to the powerful digital systems we use today. Now, with quantum computing on the horizon, we are standing at the edge of a new revolution—one that could change the way we solve problems, process information, and even understand the world around us.

But what does this future look like? Will quantum computers become as common as smartphones, or will they remain specialized tools for scientists and governments? How will they reshape industries, security, and daily life? As we look ahead, one thing is certain: quantum computing is not just about faster calculations—it is about redefining what is possible.

Will classical computers become obsolete?

With the rise of quantum computing, a common question arises: **Will classical computers eventually disappear?** The simple answer is **no**. Instead of replacing classical computers, quantum computers will complement them by handling specific types of problems that classical machines struggle with.

To understand why classical computers will remain relevant, it's important to recognize their strengths. Today's computers are highly efficient at performing everyday tasks: sending emails, browsing the internet, running business applications, and processing multimedia. They work reliably, are widely available, and do not require extreme conditions to function. Quantum computers, on the other hand, are fundamentally different. They rely on quantum mechanics to process information in ways that classical computers cannot, but they are not superior in every aspect.

Quantum computers excel in areas such as simulating molecules for drug discovery, optimizing supply chains, and breaking encryption codes. These are highly specialized tasks that classical computers struggle with. However, quantum machines are not well-suited for word processing, video editing, or running a website—tasks that classical computers perform efficiently.

A useful comparison is the relationship between airplanes and cars. Airplanes revolutionized long-distance travel, but they did not replace cars. Each serves a different purpose, and both continue to coexist. Similarly, quantum computers will become powerful tools in specific fields, while classical computers will remain the foundation of personal, business, and industrial computing.

Another key factor is practicality. Most quantum computers today require ultra-cold temperatures close to absolute zero, as well as highly controlled environments to function. This makes them impractical for everyday users. Even as technology advances and quantum computers become more accessible, they will still be expensive and specialized. It is unlikely that people will have quantum laptops or smartphones anytime soon.

Instead of making classical computers obsolete, quantum technology is likely to **enhance** them. Researchers are already exploring hybrid computing systems that combine classical and quantum elements, allowing them to work together for maximum efficiency.

In the foreseeable future, we will continue to rely on classical computers for most applications. Quantum computers will play a growing role in solving complex scientific and industrial problems, but they will not replace the machines we use daily. Rather than a competition, the future of computing will be about **coexistence**, where each technology is used for what it does best.

The latest developments

Recent advancements in quantum computing have pushed the technology closer to real-world applications, with major players making significant breakthroughs in chip design and computational efficiency. Companies such as Amazon, Microsoft, and Google are leading the way, each introducing innovations aimed at improving quantum hardware and accelerating the timeline for practical quantum solutions.

Amazon has revealed a new quantum processor, designed to enhance efficiency in quantum error correction. One of the biggest challenges in quantum computing is maintaining stable calculations despite interference from external factors. This new chip takes a novel approach by leveraging advanced qubit designs that significantly reduce the need for traditional error correction methods. This improvement makes it easier to scale quantum systems while maintaining accuracy.

Microsoft has also made a major breakthrough with a new quantum chip that introduces an innovative method for stabilizing qubits. By using a specialized material that enables greater control over quantum states, this chip is expected to make quantum computations more reliable and scalable. Experts believe that this development brings the technology closer to solving large-scale industrial problems, from financial modeling to pharmaceutical research.

Meanwhile, Google has announced an ambitious plan to bring quantum computing into commercial applications within the next five years. While many experts had predicted that practical applications were still decades away, Google's accelerated timeline signals growing confidence in the field. If successful, this could lead to quantum technologies being integrated into industries much sooner than expected.

These recent advancements highlight the rapid progress being made in the field. While quantum computing is still in its early stages, the improvements in hardware and stability suggest that real-world applications are on the horizon. Over the next few years, we may witness quantum computing transition from experimental research to a tool capable of solving some of the world's most complex challenges.

The next steps in quantum research

Quantum computing has already made remarkable progress, but there is still a long way to go before it reaches its full potential. The technology is in its early stages, much like classical computers were in the mid-20th century. To move forward, researchers are focusing on several key areas to improve quantum computers and make them more practical.

One of the biggest challenges is **error correction**. Quantum computers are incredibly powerful in theory, but they are also extremely delicate. The quantum bits, or qubits, that store information are easily disturbed by their environment, leading to errors in calculations. Unlike classical computers, which have well-developed error correction methods, quantum systems need new ways to detect and fix mistakes without disturbing the fragile quantum state. Scientists are actively working on this, developing techniques to make quantum computations more reliable.

Another major goal is **increasing the number of stable qubits**. Today's most advanced quantum computers have only a few hundred qubits, but experts believe that we will need millions of high-quality qubits to unlock the full power of quantum computing. Researchers are exploring new materials and technologies to build better qubits that last longer and make fewer errors.

Improving **hardware and scalability** is also a crucial step. Right now, most quantum computers operate under extreme conditions, often requiring temperatures close to absolute zero. This makes them expensive and difficult to maintain. Future research aims to create more practical and energy-efficient quantum systems that can work at higher temperatures and be integrated into everyday technology. Some researchers are even exploring **room-temperature quantum computing**, which could make quantum technology far more accessible.

Another area of development is **quantum algorithms**. Even if we build more powerful quantum computers, they will only be useful if we know how to program them effectively. Researchers are designing new quantum algorithms to tackle problems in medicine, finance, artificial intelligence, and cybersecurity. As we develop better ways to use quantum computers, their real-world applications will expand.

One of the most exciting possibilities is **quantum networking**. Scientists are working on building quantum communication systems that use the principles of quantum mechanics to transmit data in a highly secure way. This could eventually lead to a "quantum internet," where information is exchanged with unprecedented levels of security.

Finally, collaboration between **governments, private companies, and universities** will play a key role in the future of quantum research. Countries around the world are investing billions into quantum technology, recognizing its potential to transform industries and national security. Major tech companies and startups are also competing to develop the next breakthroughs, bringing together some of the brightest minds in physics, computer science, and engineering.

The coming decades will be crucial for quantum computing. As research progresses, we will see quantum machines become more powerful, reliable, and useful. While it may take years before they become a regular part of our lives, the work being done today is laying the foundation for a future where quantum computing reshapes science, business, and technology.

The long-term vision

Quantum computing is still in its early days, but looking ahead, its impact on the world could be as revolutionary as the invention of electricity or the internet. The long-term vision of quantum computing is not just about making computers faster—it's about opening doors to discoveries and technologies that we cannot even fully imagine yet.

One of the most significant possibilities is **solving problems that are impossible for classical computers**. Today, many scientific and technological challenges take too long to compute, even with the most advanced supercomputers. Quantum computers could change that by processing complex calculations in seconds instead of thousands of years. This could lead to breakthroughs in material science, where new superconductors or ultra-efficient batteries could be designed. It could also revolutionize medicine, making it possible to simulate molecules and develop new drugs with unmatched speed and accuracy.

Another long-term goal is **transforming artificial intelligence**. AI has already made incredible progress, but training deep learning models takes massive amounts of data and computing power. Quantum computers could process vast amounts of information in parallel, making AI systems much more powerful and efficient. This could lead to smarter automation, better decision-making, and even AI that can learn and evolve in ways we can't yet predict.

Global security and encryption will also be affected. Today's encryption methods, which protect everything from online banking to military communications, could eventually be broken by quantum computers. This is both a challenge and an opportunity. Scientists are already developing new forms of quantum encryption that would be nearly impossible to hack. In the future, we may see the rise of an ultra-secure "quantum internet" that ensures absolute privacy in communication.

As quantum technology matures, we may also see **new industries emerge**. Just as classical computing led to the internet, smartphones, and artificial intelligence, quantum computing could give birth to fields that we haven't even thought of yet. Imagine financial models that can predict global economic shifts with unprecedented accuracy, or climate simulations that can precisely forecast and help prevent natural disasters.

However, with these possibilities come important **ethical and philosophical questions**. Who will control quantum computing? Will it be available to everyone, or will only a few powerful corporations and governments have access? How will we ensure that this technology benefits humanity rather than being used for harmful purposes? These are questions that researchers, policymakers, and society as a whole must consider as we move toward a quantum future.

The long-term vision of quantum computing is filled with both promise and responsibility. While we may not yet know exactly how this technology will shape the world, one thing is certain: it has the potential to redefine the way we understand and interact with reality itself. The journey is just beginning, and the future is full of possibilities.

WHAT'S NEXT?

Thank you for joining me on this journey through the fascinating world of Quantum Computing. I truly hope you enjoyed reading this book and found it insightful and rewarding.

If you did, I would deeply appreciate it if you could take a moment to share your thoughts by leaving a review. Reviews not only help other readers discover the book but also inspire me to continue writing and exploring new topics.

To leave a review:

1. Visit the book's page online.
2. Scroll down to the **Customer Reviews** section.
3. Click the button that says **Write a Customer Review** and share your experience.

Your support means the world to me and will fuel my motivation to write even more books for you.

ABOUT THE AUTHOR

Tyler Soloway holds a Master's degree in Computer Science and has been at the forefront of artificial intelligence innovation since 2011. With over a decade of experience as an AI Engineer, he has worked across diverse fields, including Machine Learning, Prompt Engineering, Generative AI, Large Language Models (LLMs), and AI Agents.

Tyler Soloway writes about computer science, artificial intelligence, and trading in financial markets, striving to make complex topics both engaging and accessible to a wide audience.

Feel free to visit the author's page to stay updated on new releases covering science, technology, trading, and investing.

Alternatively, you can use the web link below:

https://www.amazon.com/stores/Tyler-Soloway/author/B0DT1MZZLL

SOURCES

The first draft of this book was completed in March 2025. It reflects the personal views and expertise of the author, an Artificial Intelligence (AI) Engineer with over a decade of experience, beginning in 2011. The author has worked extensively in areas such as Machine Learning, Prompt Engineering, Generative AI, Large Language Models (LLMs), Retrieval-Augmented Generation (RAG), AI Agents, and Cloud technologies, particularly AWS.

This book is not just a product of knowledge and experience but also a testament to the collaborative potential between human creativity and AI technology. AI was used responsibly as a companion to enhance the writing process, producing high-quality content and providing an engaging experience for the reader. It's important to note that while AI played a supportive role, it did not replace the author's voice or creative input. Instead, it served to augment the writing process, illustrating how AI can empower writers rather than substitute them.

To ensure transparency, the author is open about how AI technology was utilized throughout the book's creation. Below is an outline of the tools and their specific roles:

- **ChatGPT**: Used during various stages of the writing process, including idea generation, manuscript outlining, topic research, content drafting, grammar and spelling checks, and stylistic improvements. The entire manuscript underwent a thorough manual review and was edited extensively to align with the author's unique voice and style.

- **QuillBot.com**: Used primarily for grammar and spelling checks. Occasionally, it was employed to rephrase certain sentences and refine the writing style for clarity and readability.

- **Originality.ai**: Used to verify the originality of the book's content and manage the risk of unintentional plagiarism, especially in sections involving AI-generated content.

It is worth noting that tools like Originality.ai, widely recognized in the industry for AI detection, flagged this book as 100% AI-generated. This includes sections entirely written by the author without any AI assistance. The reason lies in the workflow: every part of the book was reviewed using AI tools such as ChatGPT and QuillBot.com to refine the style and enhance the reader's experience.

This section underscores the careful integration of AI in the creative process - an approach that showcases how technology can amplify human creativity while maintaining transparency and integrity.

www.ingramcontent.com/pod-product-compliance
Lightning Source LLC
La Vergne TN
LVHW041211050326
832903LV00021B/576